CONCEPTUAL MANAGEMENT

How to Convert Life Experiences to
Effective Management Techniques

JOHN E. BAKER JR

PUBLISHED BY FIDELI PUBLISHING, INC.

ISBN: 978-1-60414-939-5

For information, please contact
Fideli Publishing, Inc.:
info@fidelipublishing.com
www.FideliPublishing.com

ABOUT THE AUTHOR

John Baker is the Vice President of Manufacturing for a contract manufacturing company in Racine, Wisconsin. Born in 1954, he earned a B.S. degree in Engineering and Economics in 1996 from the University of Wisconsin, Parkside, and an MBA from Cardinal Stritch University in 2012. He and his wife have three grown children and two granddaughters.

John started in manufacturing in 1973 and soon realized that there was more to manufacturing than producing a product. He also recognized that by improving the overall process, the product improved. During his early years, John studied numerous production methods by running the process and later by supervising different production areas.

In 1983, John entered college, hoping to acquire further education that could be used in conjunction with the hands-on know-how derived from working. By combining the two different methods of learning, John was promoted several times and gained additional experience. Seeing that more schooling would aid him in his career goals, he went back to school again to earn his MBA. John received his MBA in 2012 and was promoted to VP of Manufacturing.

During this time, John's involvements included labor negotiations; legal matters, both as a company defendant and a witness; process improvements; and establishing new directions for the company, which continue today.

John knew that, even after taking all of this action, he was not done learning. John wrote down some of the lessons that he learned. By reviewing these early lessons, it was easy to see how they related to management techniques. He found twists in other lessons that at the time seemed unapparent, unclear, and painful in some cases, but in the end, different learning paths illuminated successful management traits.

These traits, all of which John gleaned from his own personal conflicts, interactions with a wide variety of people and environments, and the blending of his education with life experiences, will be enumerated in this book. All of this formal or informal training taught managerial skills, but it also helped with life itself.

ACKNOWLEDGMENTS

I would like to thank my wife Mary for her endless love and support as I have faced challenges in my life. She has been with me through all of my learning experiences.

I would also like to thank my mother-in-law and father-in-law. Even though they have passed on, their lessons and wisdom remain with me every day.

Thanks to my three children, Carly, Jessica, and John. Their adventures growing up added to my joy as we all learned together.

I am indebted to Ernie and Bernice Styberg for allowing me the chance to study and grow with their company. This includes my cohorts along the way, such as Mike Budish and the late Ron Jones, as well as others.

Lastly, thank you to Jolie and Lilie, my grand-angels.

CONTENTS

PART I
MANAGEMENT BEGINS

PART II
SECOND SEASON

PART III
ASSEMBLE YOUR KNOWLEDGE

PREFACE

As defined in the Encarta dictionary, a manager is *somebody who is responsible for directing and controlling the work and staff of a business, or of a department within it.*[41] Most people think that management skills are achieved either on-the-job or in the classroom, but that is not exactly correct. Management skills start at a much younger age.

Numerous discussions, articles, and opinions attempt to explain whether people are motivated to be first-rate managers or leaders or whether people may learn these skills as they need them. I will try to determine an answer to that question from a different vantage point here.

An abundance of reasons exist why this continues to be a challenging question, as the answer is not obvious or easily understood. The answer depends on the person and the environment in which the person finds himself. In this book, I will provide you with examples of different types of environments that I hope will lead to a conclusion about what makes a capable manager.

PART I

MANAGEMENT BEGINS

1

INITIAL STAGES OF MANAGEMENT

Good management is the art of making problems so interesting and their solutions so constructive that everyone wants to get to work and deal with them. — Paul Hawken

CHAPTER PREVIEW

1

Management traits develop long before a person decides to become a manager.

2

Social conditions affect personnel far more than a new manager would think.

3

Finding and keeping employees is becoming difficult.

In this book I take a different approach to explaining management skills and the knowledge needed to be an accomplished manager. By reviewing certain events in my life and how those events relate to management skills, I will establish a connection that will show that management skills are learned early in life.

I will illustrate that some of our early experiences help cultivate management skills. It all depends upon how we use life's experiences as they relate to management.

This does not mean that every manager must go through events similar to those that this author went through, but these past events will assist me in proving that skills in management are fostered at an earlier age than traditionally considered.

In my case, lessons began at a young age. Growing up in the 1950s in poverty, with a single mother, painted my world in a negative way. Single, divorced mothers were viewed as an indication of a low-class family. Even at 5 years old, I could sense that this would not bode well for me.

Going to elementary school and seeing my classmates' mothers looking at me as someone with whom they did not want their children to play was hard and confusing.

My age made the situation difficult. Being so young I did not imagine that I was learning a valuable lesson in discrimination. I soon found out that being polite and courteous went further than being mean and tough.

Not being very smart, I had to work hard to learn. Unfortunately, I did not get a lot of help at home. My mother worked tirelessly to keep a roof over our heads, but she did not finish high school herself, so teaching her children was not within her area of expertise. This is not to say that I did not appreciate my mother. I did, but this lack of formal educational opportunities at home hindered me, as will be seen in the following chapters.

Not everyone comes from the same background. This creates differences in learning skills, culture, and social behavior. As a new or future manager, it behooves you to remember that not everyone learns at the same pace. Attempts have been made to improve educational methods at all age levels, however, a manager should never assume that any education outside the company's own training program was as beneficial as necessary. Assume the worst, but be pleased when someone shows more evidence of knowledge than what may have first been perceived.

To take this point a step further, let's review a case of discrimination, learning, and social opinions by examining an example of affirmative action: an article written by Nathan Glazer, an American sociologist who taught at the University of California at Berkeley and for more than twenty years at Harvard and is known for his opinions and writings about domestic policies.[48]

In Glazer's article *In Defense of Preference* he focuses on affirmative action:

> As defenders of affirmative action often point out, paper-and-pencil tests of information, reading comprehension, vocabulary, reasoning, and the like are not perfect indicators of individual ability. But they are the best measures we have for success in college and professional schools.[88]

As Glazer noted and believed, referring to civil right laws of 1964, *today, a vast gulf of difference persists between the educational and occupational status of blacks and whites.*

Another view was taken as related to the *melting pot.* The melting pot is a concept that explained that by taking different groups of people (race or gender), companies and learning institutions alike would benefit because there would be a wider range of views/comments expressed due to the different experiences of each individual. This would improve the overall knowledge of all involved.

This melting pot concept was the general theme of an article written by Francesca Biller, an award-winning investigative journalist.[9] When conducting random interviews for this article, the author interviewed a cross-section of people from different racial and ethnic groups.

One such person was Ken Wesley, an African-American male with a Masters degree in E-Business and owner of a photography business, who had an interesting view. *I see America as more of a salad bowl, allowing each individual to maintain his or her own presence and uniqueness, yet still con-*

> **"**
>
> **Not everyone comes from the same background. This creates differences in learning skills, culture, and social behavior.**
>
> **"**

tributing to the overall goodness of this nation as a whole.[9]

Education as a whole benefits from the diversity of views from students with different backgrounds in a class.[57]

A third view was documented by James Traub, an author with a focus on politics and international affairs with credits at *The New York Times*, *The New Yorker*, and more, as well as his own five books, and who has written profiles about Barack Obama, Al Gore, and John McCain as well as being a member of the Council on Foreign Relations.[123]

Traub states in his article *Testing Texas* that a range of statistical numbers depict dropout rates after students enter college, but all of these numbers are after-effects because when evaluating these numbers, it is already too late to change or improve the conditions.[123]

As Auren Hoffman, CEO of Rapleaf, a reputation management company, pointed out, "*To solve the problems of affirmative action, low college entrance scores, and educational differences, people need to get to the heart of the issue and teach students to reach for college-performance education at the kindergarten level.*"[57]

Affirmative action's intent was noble, but with the recent news concerning high school education test scores in the United States, it emphasizes that all of the affirmative action will not help the problem highlighted in James Traub's article.[88,97]

Why do the above points matter? If education is not effective at the grade school level, a hiring manager cannot assume what people know even after high school, which is a concern today.

A manager must be aware that, in numerous cases, a new hire did not cause his own academic level, but the new hire and the employer both must live with the social and environmental conditions that may hinder a new employee. Employees newly hired may have a much different level of education than people already hired and trained within an organization.

As noted above, people are different and come from a variety of social places and races, so managers must be aware of individual differences and be willing to try to understand those differences. In some cases, as stated above, people from varying backgrounds may produce a melting pot effect by co-mingling viewpoints, ideas, and suggestions raised in the workplace due to their own diverse backgrounds, while keeping their own sense of pride in the process.

My social skills and educational level were sorely lacking when I was originally hired at ABC Engineering Company, but after working hard and taking advantage of the learning opportunities given to me by my employer, I made countless progressive steps.

It is unfortunate that the unemployment rate was high in 2013, a 7.5 percent average for ten months in the United States. However, at the same time, jobs were available, but prospects could not pass a simple set of tests or lacked the minimum social skills needed to fill the positions.

Understanding the above conditions, companies have reduced their minimum hiring requirements where need be, hoping that between an individual's willingness to learn and a company that is willing to be patient, new skill sets for employees may be obtained through training.

This practice has taken a lot of management time and understanding, and the results have been a 40 to 50 percent success rate. The raw data indicates that out of fifty resumes, eight people pass the first interview, four are hired, and within one year, two people will still be employed.[35] Those people who do make it are normally excellent employees, so with perseverance, the company may hire employees worth keeping. However, as noted above, lack of education and social differences need to be addressed now and way before people enter the workforce.[35]

CHAPTER 1
ASSESSMENT

1. **When do management traits start?** Individuals may note that management traits start as early as grade school age, if they think back, those thoughts may be useful at times.

2. **How should managers prepare for new personnel?** Training must be broken down into the least complicated formula for any given job. Recall that the caliber of personnel hired will vary widely, and not necessarily by an individual's choice but by social skills already learned. Companies must adjust training to make sure that it makes sense for all individuals hired.

3. **Are there benefits inherent in the melting pot and/or salad bowl effects?** Yes. The melting pot concept allows the blending of the previous experiences of all personnel to bring new vision into an organization from different viewpoints, while the individual keeps her own sense of heritage and pride. But management must ask, listen, and draw the vision out of the individuals that it hires.

4. **What should managers be aware of, more than a resume, when hiring individuals?** The social make-up of the community and how individuals from the community are affected. A company may have to adjust to these conditions. This may not be seen through a resume, but through the people whom a company hires.

CHAPTER CHALLENGE

Write a list of five examples and describe proof of the ways in which the melting pot/salad bowl effect may be beneficial.

2

KNOWLEDGE

> *If a man empties his purse into his head, no one can take it away from him. An investment in knowledge always pays the best interest.* — Benjamin Franklin

CHAPTER PREVIEW

1

There are differences between knowledge and motivation.

2

People need to be able to acquire knowledge.

3

Knowledge encourages problem prevention.

Never underestimate a youngster. Even in my first two to three years of school, I learned meaningful lessons. I first learned to study with my eyes and not my mouth. Even a task such as tying shoelaces may be monumental for a child. I watched and studied two classmates over and over until I got this myself.

At this point, we must ask whether one comes by management skills because of knowledge or motivation. Of course, this question has no one correct answer. Under different sets of conditions, the answer varies. To understand which is more important, we must recognize the differences between knowledge and motivation. One set of definitions states that knowledge is wealth, whereas motivation is built on the bricks of optimism and confidence.[108]

With that said, knowledge is gained by studying and learning, and acquiring knowledge helps one to become successful. Circumstances pop up everyday where having knowledge may make a situation easier to deal with. This could be as elementary as filling a bicycle tire with air.

Knowledge helps prevent a person from putting too much air into the tire. With knowledge, one would know that if they put too much air into the tire, the tire would pop. Not only listening to others, but watching others allows one to gain additional knowledge.

It is knowledge that helps one to pick the direction necessary to thrive and conquer. As above, knowledge is wealth, because the

> "...knowledge is gained by studying and learning. Acquiring knowledge helps one become successful.

more that is learned, the more that knowledge may be used to achieve personal goals.

As told in Jeffrey A. Mello's book *Strategic Human Resource Management*, a firefighter was caught in a forest fire and had the knowledge that if he built a small, separate fire and then stayed in the area of this fire, this would protect him from the forest fire that was approaching, whereas his fellow firefighters did not possess this knowledge. All of the other firefighters perished in the forest fire.[88]

Knowledge saved this firefighter's life. Knowledge is the information that has been absorbed by an individual. Exams exist that test knowledge. These IQ tests test people's overall knowledge. Different types of tests are available to determine someone's IQ, and these tests tend to measure a wide range of knowledge, but all are designed to discover what a person can recall.[92]

CHAPTER 2
ASSESSMENT

1. **Why should one acquire knowledge?** It aids in preventing spiraling out of control.

2. **Does the knowledge of a manager improve control of personnel?** Yes. With knowledge a manager may tend to the needs of personnel. However, knowledge will not take care of all predicaments. A competent manager knows when to seek the counsel of others, if necessary.

CHAPTER CHALLENGE

Choose and write about a businessperson that you know who uses knowledge and wisdom to provide exemplary counsel to others.

3

MOTIVATION

CHAPTER PREVIEW

1

Motivation is difficult to measure..

2

Motivation may take people beyond their own limits.

3

Motivation improves training.

Another thing that I dealt with as a child, and still live with today, is color blindness. Color blindness is a disability, but it is hard for a 6-year-old to understand why colors look different to everyone else, so I figured out how to get around the disability and flourish. I learned what colors items were supposed to be. Soon after, I learned to read the names of colors written on crayons. Tree leaves are green whereas a tree trunk is brown, so I looked for the words green and brown on a crayon and used this information as necessary. By studying and watching others, I became proficient. At that age, my motivation was to avoid embarrassment.

Motivation is not as easy to explain as knowledge. Motivation is primarily based on emotion from external influences.[108]

Motivation may be seen in the trials of someone who failed at two businesses, ran for public office four times, and had a nervous breakdown, ultimately becoming the president of the United States. Who is this person? Abraham Lincoln.[108]

> **Motivation is the reason why people go beyond everyday requirements...**

Abraham Lincoln said, "The probability that we may fail in the struggle ought not to deter us from the support of a cause we believe to be just; it shall not deter me."[52]

As Abraham Lincoln proved, nothing held him back.

Motivation and knowledge feed off of each other. This topic became the basis of a study conducted by Georgetown University student, Victor Clough. The study was conducted to prove whether motivation or knowledge plays a greater role in the productivity of personnel. The second purpose of the study was to evaluate what the different knowledge levels were before the computer training sessions and then to determine who benefited the most.

The study was done at a workplace with the five hundred and fifty people participating being evaluated for promotability. It measured workplace and computer skills prior to any training. Then data was collected from these people via course evaluations after a computer training session. This data came from fifty separate learning events, in twelve geographical locations throughout the U.S.

The feedback from the evaluations was used to draw conclusions about personal motivation as compared to knowledge levels before the training course.

The pre-course workplace and computer skills measurements were then compared to evaluations gathered after the training sessions were completed. This was done on an individual by individual basis. The results showed that those who entered the training session with more motivation than knowledge exceeded their own expectations.

Clough monitored the inverse as well. The study showed that people who had high levels of subject knowledge prior to the training session, but little motivation, did not expect much of themselves at the completion of the computer training session. The end results were that knowledge levels evened out, so motivation did play a key factor when external demands helped drive people to try.[27]

I comprehended at a young age that just getting by was not going to be enough. Being a poor child who put cardboard in my shoes to protect my feet from stones and rain gave me insight. It helped me to cultivate a true appreciation of what I did not want in the future, and I knew at that time that I needed to do more.

A manager must first be a motivator. In order to motivate, a manager must look at each individual, see what that person needs and wants, and determine what may be done to assist the individual in achieving the most that they can possibly achieve.

Groups of individuals such as teams, departments, and even work-related shifts all may demonstrate subtle differences that come down to the manager motivating both the group and the individual within the groups. Even though the ability to motivate is needed in order for a manager to

> **Motivation creates a desire in managers to learn more, so motivation and knowledge are inseparable.**

effectively lead her team, a manager must acquire some knowledge first. Some knowledge may have allowed the manager to earn her managerial position, but that thirst for knowledge must not stop. Managers must augment their knowledge as they grow into their positions.

Motivation creates a desire in managers to learn more, so motivation and knowledge are inseparable. Some new managers may think that some day, after enough knowledge is acquired and motivation is at a fine level, they can sit back and enjoy a job well done. But if that thought enters his mind, a seasoned manager should worry. A manager must know that he can never let his guard down and rest on his laurels — he must always strive to improve.

As stated above, knowledge is necessary. However, knowledge may be taught whereas motivation may not. To be motivated and to be able to motivate others is a gift. A person who is true to him or herself cannot fake motivation. Some might think they can fake it, but others see right through them.

Motivation is the reason why people go beyond everyday requirements, and those who are motivated tend to help others become more motivated by their own actions. Sometimes people motivate others but never know that they are doing it because motivation may be not what is said but what is done that is seen by others.

This is especially true with new employees. New employees tend to be open to learning and watching others within the organization. It is during this time that it becomes apparent to the new employee which employees and managers are motivated in their jobs. A manager must truly believe in her job, and if she does, her motivation will rub off on others.

CHAPTER 3
ASSESSMENT

1. **Which is more important, knowledge or motivation?** A manager may be knowledgeable but not motivated, so there is a chance that he will go nowhere. A manager who is highly motivated but lacks knowledge will most likely struggle. A qualified manager needs both knowledge and motivation.

2. **What may be seen but not measured?** Motivation may be seen if one knows what to look for, but is difficult to measure.

3. **One cannot teach motivation, so how may it be achieved?** Motivated people create motivation in others.

CHAPTER CHALLENGE

Find and write about one company that broadcasts (articles, news, books) the motivational skills of its managers.

4

TALENT

> *Some people can do one thing magnificently, like Michelangelo, and others make things like semiconductors or build 747 airplanes — that type of work requires legions of people. In order to do things well, that can't be done by one person, you must find extraordinary people.* — Steve Jobs

CHAPTER PREVIEW

1	**2**	**3**
Take the time to find capable talent.	People want and need rewards (but not necessarily money).	Talent is all around you, but you must look for it.

While managers are motivating, they should keep an eye open for those individuals who show that *something extra*. With the idea of promoting from within, all managers need to take the time to look closely at each person with whom they work. If managers take a bit of time, it may become apparent which employees give that something extra and seem to be on top of what they are assigned to do. Managers should then add these individuals to the future promotion list. It may take a lot of time before these employees become promotable, but during that time, management should inspire these individuals to continue to learn.

Clayton Alderfer, a psychologist who wrote an alternative theory of human needs in the late 1960s, believed that human beings have a desire to grow and to use their abilities to their fullest potential, and he also believed that managers should customize their reward and recognition programs to meet employees' varying needs.[71]

This means that when an employee shows that she has more to offer, the manager must take steps to encourage her. This allows management to see if the individual has what it takes when given more responsibility, but time must be taken to slowly allow the person to show her abilities. In most cases, everyone wins. A manager should keep a list of promotable employees who could fill management roles when they open up.

> **The observant manager sees which employees' skills are developing, like a seed planted in a garden...**

The observant manager sees which employees' skills are developing, like a seed planted in a garden, and the individual may see that she is growing as well. If problems do occur, changes may be made before the individual or the company looks bad. A manager should always keep a running personnel promotion list.[35]

CHAPTER 4
ASSESSMENT

1. **Why waste time looking at an individual's potential?** Managers do not have the time to waste, right? This is how some managers tend to view employee potential, but the return on investment is well worth keeping an eye on key personnel.

2. **How may a manager tell ahead of time if a person will work out in another position?** Find those individuals with talent, and give them a taste of having additional responsibility without any pressure. A clever manager will help before any serious problems arise.

CHAPTER CHALLENGE

Many stories have been told about finding hidden talent. Find and write about a case of a manager finding an unexpected gold mine of talent.

5

JOB SATISFACTION

> *I think the foremost quality — there's no success without it — is really loving what you do. If you love it, you do it well, and there's no success if you don't do well what you're working at.* — Malcolm Forbes

CHAPTER PREVIEW

1

People want to believe in and then improve on satisfaction.

2

Motivating people may improve satisfaction.

3

Maslow's Hierarchy of Needs is genuine.

The ultimate goal for a manager is to create job satisfaction for all employees. This may sound easy, but accomplishing this may seem impossible. A manager may satisfy one person, but the goal is to satisfy all members of the group.

As famous football coach Vince Lombardi once said, "The achievements of an organization are the results of the combined effort of each individual."[75]

The same holds true of job satisfaction, no matter what the occupation. When a person who believes in an organization makes a difference through affirmative suggestions, he will feel great about himself. This is the true meaning of job satisfaction. Job satisfaction of his employees also helps a manager believe that what he is trying to accomplish does matter, which in turn helps the organization become successful.

In sixth grade I had a motivated teacher, and one day he announced that he planned to have the students perform a musical and was looking for volunteers. I had never sung or acted before, but this sounded interesting to me, so I tried out. The teacher said, right up front, that he expected the best out of everyone who tried out and that the practices would be long. As a 12-year-old, I did not know what he meant, but I soon found out.

The teacher held tryouts for roles that needed to be played while other roles would be merely singing background. I earned a limited role on stage. I was ecstatic. The kids practiced over and over. If one person screwed up, the whole group had to do everything again. The teacher explained that when we performed, the group as a whole would either make or break the play, so we all needed to achieve perfection.

This was the first time that I felt that I was a member of a group outside of my own interests. We not only performed for our own school, the school district allowed us to perform the musical in an auditorium with two shows for more than nine hundred other fifth and sixth grade students.

It was then that I realized the value of motivation. Of course, I did not know at the time what motivation entailed, but I knew then what being motivated felt like.

Similarly, one noteworthy company appears to have a superb grasp of motivation, Southwest Airlines. While Southwest is marketing-based, it is plain after reviewing Southwest's management methods that its goal is to earn new customers, but it also tries to motivate employees to go beyond the normal practices to garner the attention of new and existing customers, which affects job satisfaction.[120] (This will be examined more closely in Case Study #8).

> **People *want* to go to work only if they enjoy it.**

People *want* to go to work only if they enjoy it. They enjoy their jobs if they feel that they are an integral piece of the company's puzzle. Since a company cannot run without employees doing their jobs, why not allow each employee to feel pride in the work that he does. It does require extra work from the managers to drive this message home, but it is worth it. A manager who dismisses the use of titles and puts everyone on the same team, including the manager, then has a group of people from whom she may get more.

Employees want to work for a manager who gives credit where it is due. A manager does not need to flaunt a title unless an employee is contrary (in which case, choices are limited), but otherwise, the better the team, the better an area will run, because the employees want to do a better job.[82]

As psychologist Abraham Maslow stated in his Hierarchy of Needs theory, meeting ones physiological needs, or most basic needs, such as food, water, and warmth, comes first. Second is the need for safety. Third is the need to belong. And fourth is the need to feel accomplishment.[65]

Managers would do well to follow Maslow's Hierarchy of Needs with respect to their employees. If managers make employees feel that they are doing their jobs the best that they can, this helps an employee feel smart and ensures that he feels like he is part of a team.[65] If managers manage their employees correctly, the employees feel proud of their job performance.

CHAPTER 5
ASSESSMENT

1. **How may employees become an ideal fit for the company?** Managers must open the door to opportunity for all employees. When employees see that they can help both a company and themselves, everyone wins.

2. **Why should a manager take the time to look at those who work for her?** Most people want to do an exceptional job, so a manager must recognize these employees and open the doors to advancement.

3. **People want to be satisfied with their jobs, but what does this take?** According to Maslow's Hierarchy of Needs, if managers help people to feel good about their job and their company, this gives them a grand feeling of accomplishment.

4. **What destroys productivity but is routinely overlooked?** Unhappy employees: Individuals do not do their best when they are not satisfied, and unhappy employees tend to slow down the productivity of others.

CHAPTER CHALLENGE

Find and write about a company that uses job satisfaction as a method to improve the organization.

6

TIME MANAGEMENT

He who every morning plans the transaction of the day and follows out that plan, carries a thread that will guide him through the maze of the most busy life. But where no plan is laid, where the disposal of time is surrendered merely to the chance of incidence, chaos will soon reign. — Victor Hugo

CHAPTER PREVIEW

1

Once you lose time, you can never get it back.

2

Learn the tricks that help save time.

3

The long and the short view of time management.

One of the first questions that a new manager should ask is, *How am I supposed to learn and know all of the subjects covered in this book and still do my job every day?* This would be a wise question to ask.

William P. Lauder, CEO of Estée Lauder Companies, made a comment to a group of people, referring to his staff, that was so simple yet so true, "Time is their greatest resource, and when it's gone, it's lost forever."[71]

The true value of time may not be noticed until it is gone! Likewise, time management often goes unappreciated by new managers. Effective time management may keep a manager out of trouble and help ensure that every day runs smoothly. However, inefficient use of time may guarantee that a manager will soon be in hot water and not know how to get out of it.

Time management may be viewed in many ways, but as I see it, it is best viewed from sea level or from 35,000 feet. The same landscape may appear dissimilar from two different vantage points. So it is with time management.

We will start with the 35,000-foot view, which is called the Five Rules by Kathleen M. Eisenhardt and Donald M. Suth. The Five Rules are also applicable in strategic planning,[71] which we will cover in later chapters. The Five Rules are a method by which managers may take the overhead approach in making sure that projects, programs, and systems stay on time. The rules are as follows:

1. How-to rules: Spell out key points and what is unique about the program so that people understand it and don't waste time.

2. Boundary rules: Focus on the opportunities that exist within a given project, but discuss them outside the group so that this does not influence what the group is trying to accomplish.

3. Priority rules: Help personnel rank opportunities.

4. Timing rules: Get and keep all personnel on the same page while not losing track of the company's overall goals.

5. Exit rules: Help personnel decide when the opportunity has reached its maximum point and the program is done.[104]

As may be seen here, the purpose of the Five Rules is to keep everyone from wasting time while keeping projects on schedule. This allows personnel to be more efficient and permits the company to better save time and money. The Five Rules also prevent individuals from going in circles wondering what to do next. The Five Rules work at all levels of management.

The sea level view of time management also works for all levels of management, but it is particularly key for new managers. Learning to manage people and time together is critical. Often, what seems to be an easy task may turn into a multitude of tasks that are fired at a manager in rapid succession. It becomes difficult and frustrating to prioritize all projects.

In the sea level view of management, managers may follow a rule that we will call the A, B, C Rule. This Rule calls for a manager to rank all tasks, projects, or assignments as A, B, or C.

An A task is critical. If it is not completed in a timely manner, it will costs the company money, whether because of missed shipments or sales, costs of production, upset customers, or a hit to the company's reputation.

B tasks should be considered must-do. They need to be done soon, or they may escalate to A assignments. B projects may be costly as well if not followed closely, but time is still available to take corrective measures before all hell breaks loose.

The projects that most people are comfortable doing are C projects. These tasks do not need to be completed immediately and could constitute a waste of time, such as checking e-mails as opposed to resolving a discipline problem.[13] In most cases, the e-mails can wait.

The biggest problem with the A, B, C Rule is discipline. Without even being aware of it, most people will automatically work on their C tasks while their A and B tasks sit on their desks and soon become unavoidable problems.

I witnessed poor time management first-hand in our engineering department, which had different functions, such as designing machines and processes and customizing part tooling, but the same department was also required to provide quotes for new jobs.

While designing parts and processes is normally a B task, quoting new work is an A task. If a company does not provide quotes within a short time frame, the customer will likely go elsewhere. It is not fun quoting new work, and it can be time consuming, so the engineers did not like to do it. This caused quotes to sit around until the customer called to ask for them.

At that point, customers became upset and went somewhere else. Occasionally a customer gave us one last chance, but most times, the company lost the customer. Even though the engineers understood what needed to be done, they tended to go to their comfort zone.

You must be aware of what you are doing all day and ask yourself if you need to do something now or whether an assignment may be done later. You may find that you will be able to combine tasks without causing any backups. That is when you get that you are performing unnecessary C tasks, and you must force yourself to go back to more significant projects.

Automobile maintenance may be used as a metaphor for the A, B, C Rule. One must check the tire pressure, change the oil, and wash the car. A review of these three items shows that the A, B, C Rule applies here.

Checking the tires would be an A task, as low tire pressure not only reduces gas mileage, it is dangerous. This is an easy task to accomplish, but people generally do not do it.

> **You must be aware of what you are doing all day and ask yourself if you need to do something now or whether an assignment may be done later.**

Changing the oil would be a B project. Often one has time to get this done, but if one waits too long, the engine will suffer and fail, and then it turns into an A project.

Lastly, washing the car is easy and would be a C task.

Having a clean car does not matter as much properly maintaining a car, but since washing the car may be done leisurely on a sunny day, it tends to get done with more regularity than vehicle maintenance.

Because they may disrupt someone's schedule, checking the

tire pressure and changing the oil tend to be overlooked, so they are done late or not at all.

The same is true for a manager. If a task is hard to do, or is outside the scope of run-of-the-mill projects, managers may let it wait. The A and the B tasks are outside of the norm and take more focus to complete, so they tend to be set aside. This is an error in judgment.

Another case in point relates to a new manager in my plant. This manager had years of experience in another area of the business but not in the newly assigned area. After one month, I noticed that he was working sixty to seventy hours each week. Too many hours for one person to sustain over a long period of time, so we had a meeting to discuss his work hours.

Obviously he had a time-management problem, but what was causing this loss of time? During our discussion, it became apparent that he handled numerous activities during any given day and week, so I asked him to log his activities and the time devoted to each activity for one week. We agreed to review his log one week later.

The following week we assessed his log, and we found the items causing his headaches. Below is a chart showing the percentage of time each activity required during the week:

We then analyzed each activity. After asking the new manager a few questions, I knew what needed to be done next.

We contacted a number of customers and asked if they could group their e-mails together based on the order of importance. We also met with the company's IT personnel to see if a program could be fashioned to dump our customers' schedules directly into the company's database in order to

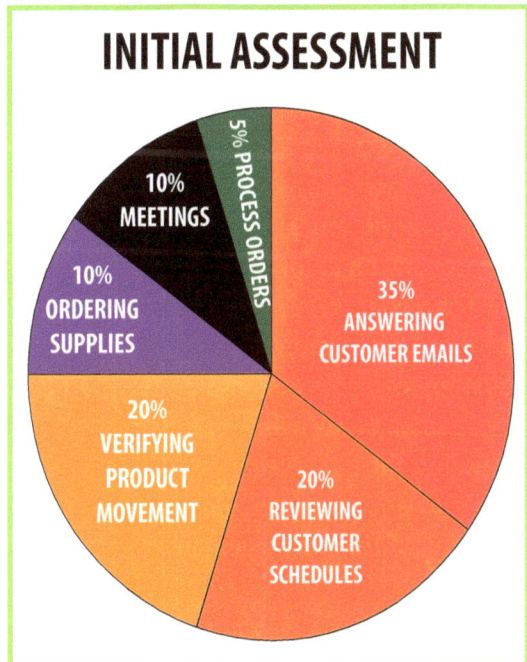

INITIAL ASSESSMENT

- 35% ANSWERING CUSTOMER EMAILS
- 20% REVIEWING CUSTOMER SCHEDULES
- 20% VERIFYING PRODUCT MOVEMENT
- 10% ORDERING SUPPLIES
- 10% MEETINGS
- 5% PROCESS ORDERS

produce a variance report from the previous week's schedule. Then the new manager could automatically adjust all schedules.

We then met with the manufacturing manager to discuss errors within the company when moving materials, and I reminded both managers that the errors were a function of the manufacturing manager and not the new manager.

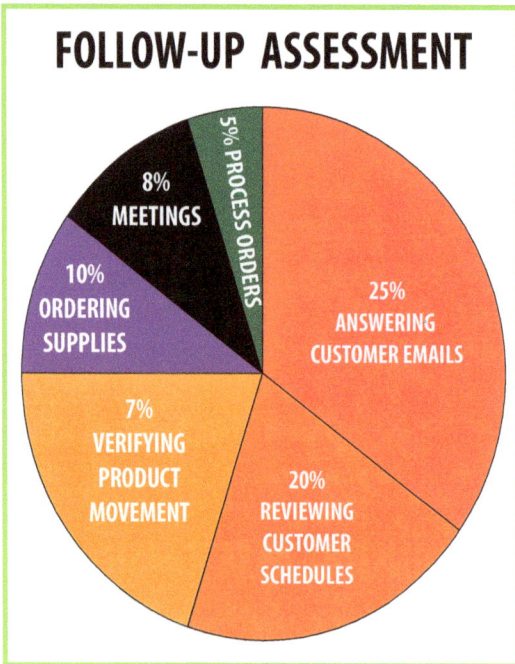

Other items led to additional discussions, and after two months, I asked the new manager to make another chart. This time the results were different:

FOLLOW-UP ASSESSMENT

- 5% PROCESS ORDERS
- 8% MEETINGS
- 10% ORDERING SUPPLIES
- 25% ANSWERING CUSTOMER EMAILS
- 7% VERIFYING PRODUCT MOVEMENT
- 20% REVIEWING CUSTOMER SCHEDULES

This new chart showed a 23 percent improvement from his original review. To improve even further upon the above numbers, the new manager is now categorizing e-mails so that critical ones are answered right away and the others are left for a later time. The company is still working on a customer schedule program, and another program is being developed to monitor supplies so that an automatic re-order system may be put into place.

I agreed to keep meetings with this manager to a minimum. As a result, the manager is more at ease and has reduced his hours. Once the above items are completed, the manager will be working more normal hours.[35]

As may be seen above, time management is evident in various applications, but the benefits may always be found if true focus is maintained. The goal is to stay out of trouble by resolving job-related challenges and avoiding burnout, so time management tools should be learned and used every day.

CHAPTER 6
ASSESSMENT

1. **The usage of time may vary from individual to group activities and is one leading cause of conflict, but it is not time that causes the conflict, rather it is how people use that time. What is the 35,000-foot view or the Five Rules?** How-to plan for success, Boundary limits for all team members, Priorities that help personnel rank opportunities, Timing to keep all employees on the same page, and Exit strategies so that everyone knows when the project is over.

2. **Why is the A, B, C Rule like a person who wants to quit smoking?** A habit or a daily pattern is not easily changed. It takes a lot of willpower and attention to avoid automatic reactions to certain low-priority assignments.

3. **Soul-searching is the key to the A, B, C Rule. Why?** Knowing where a project falls requires being true to oneself and not making excuses. C tasks are not A tasks! An individual must call the assignments as they are for this approach to work. Every day each person must focus on the A projects and not fall back to the C projects.

4. **Why shouldn't individuals tackle time management by themselves?** Everyone needs to seek assistance from whomever can help with organization and in streamlining methods and to ask for feedback from others, not as a crutch but to improve one's own efficiency.

CHAPTER CHALLENGE

Find and write about a company that uses either the Five Rules or the A, B, C Rule, and determine why it works.

7

DOCUMENTATION

I hate to tell you this, but in even the very best companies, a competitive vibe of us versus them can arise. Everyone is trying to get ahead, and sometimes people will see you as a stepping-stone to get there. Protect yourself. ... Finally, build up your notes. Don't skip along hoping that everything is going to be ok. ... Use your notes as your get-out-of-jail-free card. — Gina Trapani, founder of Lifehacker

CHAPTER PREVIEW

1
Reasons to document.

2
Ways to document.

3
Documentation constitutes self-protection.

In eighth grade, I worked on a metals project and designed three wooden ducks with metal wings, but I did not submit my design to my instructor right away. One of my classmates saw my design and submitted it before I had the chance. I lost big on that one! But it was not a total loss because I still completed the project and gave the three ducks to my grandmother, who had them until the day she died.

The value here is that I learned to document my work, in a timely manner, in order to cover myself. In order to get credit for an action, I needed to document what I had done at the time that I did it. As is illustrated above, the classmate's design was a false representation of the truth. But I had not documented the real facts in time.

New managers often do not understand the magnitude of documentation, as it is not normally taught as part of the job. The first thought of many new managers is that it takes too much time to document everything. Based on my experience, I explain here what needs to be documented and why.

WHAT:

1. Reasons for discipline.

   A. Individuals who do not follow work rules and company policies.

   B. Attendance and lateness.

   C. General attitude.

   D. Comments made that are out of line, engender fear, or intimidate, such as threats.

   E. Personal conduct that appears strange, such as a person talking to themselves with no one around.

   F. Comments overheard about events that have already taken place or that will take place.

   G. Conflicts — even minor ones — that require no discipline when they occur but that may escalate in the future.

H. Projects that you suspect will not be willingly completed on time.

One example in manufacturing would be a low-quantity job in a normally high-quantity-running department. In a restaurant, it may be cleaning grease traps. No one wants to do this, but if it is not done, the sewage may back up.

2. Customer communications (if employees are directly involved with customers or a customer conflict).

A. Personal daily communications between customers and suppliers. Even minor events should be documented.

B. Events such as changes, updates, and new requirements that may be worked on ahead of time require some proof of change.

3. Personal communications not covered above.

4. Purchase orders/contracts.

5. Legal matters.

WHY:

1. **Discipline.**

A. When an individual must be disciplined, management must be sure of all facts and must believe that all disciplinary events will end up in court or arbitration, so having more details about past problems may help with building a better defense and will assist in making a more correct disciplinary decision.

B. More documented details may catch an individual not telling the truth.

C. Written details supporting what was said between management and employees makes defending discipline easier in the future.

2. **Customer communications.**

A. The faster a supplier services a customer the better the relationship will be with the customer. However, if the customer has a better memory than the supplier, the relationship could be at risk.

This does not apply only to instances of the customer being intentionally dishonest. Memories are not always flawless. If a supplier keeps better records, it may build trust with the customer, and, if need be, the supplier may point out to the customer what he said, when, where, and, in most cases, the customer's recollection will improve.

B. Documentation also allows the supplier to move on projects or programs before any final official paperwork is completed, but after trust is built. The point here is that the customer knows that the supplier is keeping accurate records. In today's business world, time is everything, so if time may be saved, business will improve.

C. Open and complete documentation may help with public relations.

D. The customer could come back days later, and by then, the facts may be fuzzy.

3. **Personal communications.**

A. Communications take place between many different people every day. Whether between management, subcontractors, or employees, all key points should be documented.

4. **Purchase orders/contracts.**

A. Customers may push for an early start date for projects, but they cannot get an actual PO in writing to the supplier for perhaps days, and days count, so a verbal commitment is given. Written documentation in telephone logs may be used as evidence that a purchase order or contract was approved by a customer and permission was given to proceed.

This, again, is a practice that should be used after customer/supplier trust has been established. This saves time in production by allowing materials to be purchased to complete orders. With today's just-in-time mentality, companies do not hold the variety of raw materials that they did in the past.

5. **Legal matters.**

   A. Managers must sometimes be able to prove what was said or done. No one knows for sure what information will be needed in one day or two years from the date of an event. In reality, documentation will likely be needed only a handful of times, but it will be crucial in those cases.

   In a case that went to federal court, I testified two years after the incident occurred. I had no idea that my notes would be so valuable, but they were worth gold.

   B. Remember, notes themselves are not evidence but are additional proof that the manager's memory is accurate and support that the event took place as documented.

HOW:

1. **Determine what needs to be documented.**

2. **Decide the best way to document:**

   A. No one way of documentation works best, however, using different methods, depending on the circumstances, may be most efficient.

   B. E-mail works best for instructional documentation. It is efficient and may be sent to multiple people at one time. E-mails may be used as legal evidence for both sides if the case goes to court.

   C. Personal notebooks work for individual notes. The information is yours and stays private. Grammar is not critical, and you may write as briefly as you want.

   D. Shorthand is not used much anymore, but one may certainly borrow from this skill, as it may not be necessary to write every word.

   E. Texting skills come in handy, such as when writing abbreviations.

F. Speed writing means forgetting the fill-in words such as adjectives, adverbs, and words normally three letters or less (in most cases).

G. Keywords are essential when documenting times, people involved, the object in question, or a reference point (a second person, location in a building, or time of day).

Examples:

- Joe built car parts while supposed to be working on 7-22-13. Mark

- Saw Steve leave work at 3:20 p.m. on 7-22-13 via the north door. Bill

- Heard Barb say that she was going to steal paper products 7-28-13. Steve

- Bill said he hurt arm at home but claimed that he was here at the same time on 7-21-13. Paul

- Scott missing from area from 10:30 to 11:00 on 7-22-13. John

> **New managers often do not understand the magnitude of documentation, as it is not normally taught as part of the job.**

The fundamental point here is that the words documented do not need to be lengthy. Keeping it brief is fine. But you may also need to decide how best to document a one thousand-word conversation into a single paragraph.[35]

CHAPTER 7
ASSESSMENT

1. **Name the five reasons why you would want to document daily events.** Discipline, customer communications, personal communications, purchase orders/contracts, legal matters.

2. **What different methods may be used when documenting events?** E-mail, Word document, hand-written notebook, shorthand, text, speed writing, keywords.

4. **Who are you protecting when you document events?** Yourself and your employer.

CHAPTER CHALLENGE

Find and write about a case in which documentation either saved the company or the lack of documentation caused a company to lose something.

8

TRAINING

> *Excellence is an art won by training and habituation. We do not act rightly because we have virtue or excellence, but we rather have those because we have acted rightly. We are what we repeatedly do. Excellence, then, is not an act but a habit.* — Aristotle

CHAPTER PREVIEW

1	**2**	**3**
Multiple techniques may be used to train employees.	Training today matters more than it did in the past.	Training must be effective.

Growing up, I was a know-it-all with poor reading and writing skills, which was partly due to a lack of teaching at home and few resources being available to me. As a student coming from a disadvantaged family, the environment could have easily been to blame for my difficulties.

By eleventh grade, it became obvious that I had learning deficiencies. Fortunately, I had an English teacher who pushed writing in every class. The teacher's emphasis was not perfect punctuation or grammar but rather thought and flow.

I still have, to this day, one paper with a note on it from that instructor. I kept this assignment for two reasons. It reminds me of how poorly I wrote (which is still embarrassing), but it also reinforces the strength that I had for constructive thoughts. I pull this assignment out from time to time to remind myself that I was able to learn from a low point in my academic career.

Teaching creates challenges because managers do not always know what each employee's past learning skills or disadvantages were, so employers must learn to adjust for various conditions.

> **For a manager, training is the key to consistency of operations, processes, and customer interactions.**

For a manager, training is the key to consistency of operations, processes, and customer interactions. Whether the training is in retail, manufacturing, or the service sectors does not matter, as each has its own opportunities. Training might also be an aid to motivation and knowledge. Training should never be underestimated or taken for granted. It is an activity that most managers would rather forego because it takes time and requires discipline.

Training itself may be handled in more than one way and for different purposes. Opinions differ about whether classroom, on-the-job, on-line, or other types of training offer the best results, however, it is up to the individual employer and the types of processes being trained to determine which method is the best.

As with older automobiles, electronics, and so on, some individuals think of training in the same way, that it is outdated and needs replacing. And now classroom training is considered old-school and ineffective.

Joshua Greenbaum, a computer programmer, system and industry analyst, consultant, and author who has published many award-winning articles on management, stated,[49] "Training in the workforce is ineffective and poses a quality threat."

He went on to suggest that classroom methods of training cannot continue.[49] Even W. Edwards Deming, an international award-winning management consultant, who helped Japan rebound after World War II, had problems with classroom training back in the 1950s. He documented an important point, in that trainees must buy into the training program and become part of the process. If that does not happen, then training will not benefit those being trained.[32]

Therefore, the method by which employees will be trained is the first decision to make before training begins. This includes the training of new managers, as they play a pivotal role in the success of the program.

When training, the instructor wants the message to be everlasting, so using the following guide-

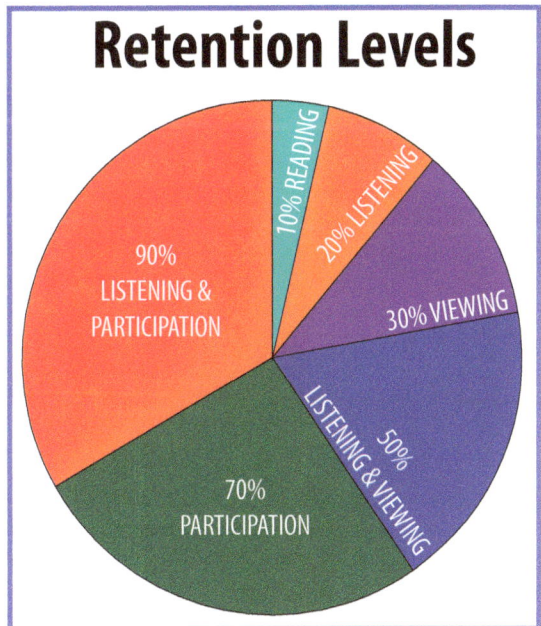

Retention Levels

- 10% READING
- 20% LISTENING
- 30% VIEWING
- 50% LISTENING & VIEWING
- 70% PARTICIPATION
- 90% LISTENING & PARTICIPATION

lines assures that individuals will effectively recall information long after the training is complete. Below are several reasons why different types of training methods are used and why:

The instructor is also key to the outcome of a training program. An instructor must keep the attention of the trainees. This is not an easy task, so the instructor must have knowledge of the subject as well as a sufficiently entertaining and informative delivery. A manager must judge carefully who the instructor will be and should not make this decision lightly.

One reason for training might be to introduce a new purpose within an organization. Companies sometimes need to revitalize their philosophies, and what better way to do this than by offering a new internal training program?

An illustration of this may be found in General Electric's past CEO Jack Welch's dominating Six Sigma program. Company personnel received job-specialized training. Some training was in the classroom, and some was on-the-job. At the end of the training, the trainee had to qualify their knowledge.[88] Qualifying gave new life to employee motivation and vastly improved quality and production levels.

Six Sigma brought a new plan to General Electric that made employees look at programs, procedures, and policies within the whole GE umbrella and allowed them to be changed.

Olive Garden utilizes training for multiple benefits by sending its chefs to training at the Culinary Institute of Tuscany, which it then advertises. When you look at the menu or view the website, Olive Garden boasts about the fact that numerous chefs are trained at the Tuscany Institute.[101] This program sends a message that Olive Garden values its customers by training its chefs to pay attention to product quality in order to deliver the delicious and consistent product their customers expect every time.

A second reason for training (which has been seen often in the years 2008 through 2016) is to re-build companies and to re-train employees of these businesses. On June 17, 2011, *IMPO* magazine reported General Motors indicated GM would invest $65 million in two GM plants to ramp up production and re-training.[59] Let's explore more about training in **Case Study #1.**

CHAPTER 8
ASSESSMENT

1. **What are the different teaching methods that may be used in training?** Reading, listening, viewing, participation, and a combination of two of the methods

2. **What role does the instructor play in training?** The instructor is key. The instructor may determine if the training is working and/or needs adjusting, and this is something that may not be found in a book. Instructors should get into their subject as well as sell it to their audience.

3. **What helps training achieve the most favorable outcome?** Making students accountable for their knowledge through listening and participating. The instructor then needs to assess how effective the training has been.

CHAPTER CHALLENGE

Choose and write about a training method that might work at your company, and determine why it would work.

RE-TRAIN TO RE-BUILD

CASE GOALS

1	**2**	**3**
Company management has a responsibility to employees.	Training/schooling helps everyone.	Better training equals better people and more motivation.

THOMASVILLE FURNITURE INDUSTRIES INC.
Headquarters: Thomasville, North Carolina
One of the principal employers in the area.

In 1996, 78,323 North Carolinians were employed in the furniture business. By 2006, that number was down to 52,453. Davidson County, where Thomasville is located, employed 7,315 people in 1996 and 3,279 people in 2006, which represented an employment level of the total community of 9.3 percent and 6.3 percent, respectively.[94]

The government of North Carolina and Davidson County employers realized that they each had a social responsibility to their citizens; so one way to solve the employment riddle was to educate the unemployed and further educate the employed. This concept needed to be a community-crafted program, but coming up with an idea proved to be the easy part.

Thomasville Furniture wanted to include the new community educational ideas into the Thomasville training program by way of the company's overall strategy. Key executives knew that the company was in need of repair and recognized that they had to do their part in the training and education of employees.

Thomasville was having more than training and unemployment issues. It was having trouble staying in business. Thomasville executives communicated their concerns to employees and members of the community, which included the following: China had more than tripled its furniture production in the four years leading up to 2006. Mexico's furniture industry was fragmented and depended on the U.S. market but still stole from U.S. workers via outsourcing. In 2006, companies from other countries were coming into the North Carolina area to buy U.S. companies.[88]

To combat this state of affairs, companies like Thomasville had been cutting employment, increasing production, but making lower profits, just to

> **Thomasville Furniture wanted to include the new community educational ideas into the Thomasville training program by way of the company's overall strategy.**

stay in business. In addition to all of these international concerns, Thomasville had to worry about other geographical areas within the U.S. Furniture companies in the Southwest were also a threat to the market. Las Vegas was producing a significant amount of furniture, which took business away from the east coast region.[94]

Thomasville had a few options in its arsenal, including mergers with other local furniture companies; increase branding, not as the highest quality furniture but in availability, including internationally; or a merger with a foreign firm.[94] With all of these decisions needing to be made, training could have fallen through the cracks in Thomasville's business plan reform, but it did not. Thomasville was trying to stay in business, and executives comprehended that making employees better made the company better.

Thomasville utilized a vertical production system, the steps of which are shown below, and this necessitated an in-depth training program.

1. Design furniture products, such as what may be used in Las Vegas casinos, closer to the customers buying the product.

2. Receive raw wood and rough it out.

3. Form, glue, and mold wood forms.

4. Sand the products.

5. Assemble and touch up.[94]

This was a labor-intensive program, but using the above steps, Thomasville offered outside education to its employees so that opportunities were available for workers to advance into management positions. As part of the form/glue/mold operations, Thomasville was looking for trained computer numerical controlled machinists and offered this group additional training in order to challenge personnel to move upward into other specialized jobs, including management positions.[94] In this way, employees could see that advancement was possible.

CASE STUDY 1
ASSESSMENT

1. **What is the point of training in this Case Study?** Even in hard times, something good may come of training.

2. **What responsibility does management have when a business fails, if any?** This depends upon the size of the company and its involvement with the community. However, large companies do have a social responsibility to help due to the impact that the loss of jobs may have on the community. This may mean many different things. This Case Study shows that both training within the company and outside education helped the company achieve its goals.

3. **Who won in this case?** The employees won, as they were given additional opportunities that they otherwise would not have had. The company won as well. The employees saw that they could move up in the organization, which gave individuals an incentive to put forth more effort, which then benefitted the company.

CASE STUDY #1 CHALLENGE

Find and write about another company that appeared to be doomed but that found a way to use training for the betterment of both the employees and the company.

9

QUALITY TRAINING

> *Quality is never an accident; it is always the result of high intention, sincere effort, intelligent direction and skillful execution; it represents the wise choice of many alternatives.* — William A. Foster

CHAPTER PREVIEW

1

Quality training is training but with a focus on quality needs.

2

Employees must believe in quality training.

3

Quality training is based on consistency.

One specialized area of training is in the field of quality. Over the last sixty years, quality programs have become available to enhance quality awareness and standards within organizations. These programs include the military specifications MIL-Q-9858, Total Quality Management (TQM), GM's Target For Excellence (TFE), Six Sigma, and Lean, some of which will be broken down in later chapters.

The latest quality standards as of 2016 to be utilized were the International Organization for Standardization (ISO) 9000 and the TS 16949. Many of the above standards started with automotive production but are no longer limited to just this area. Lessons learned through the above quality standards are now used by many other types of businesses, including aerospace, retail, software designers, healthcare, call centers, and more.[40]

In 1994, as the management representative at ABC Engineering Company Engineering, I was responsible for implementing and verifying that all steps of the ISO-9000 standards were being followed and maintained controls via audits, training processes, document controls, and building a team to monitor.

> **Superior training prevents errors and permits workers to produce high-quality products.**

The first step required 100 percent training of all company employees from the ground floor up. However, the real challenge was to get all personnel to buy into the program. This involved training personnel who had from one to forty years of seniority. The older employees were the more difficult individuals to train. They were set in their ways, so selling them was a test of my skills.

Our ISO-9000 team knew that the viability of this program

depended upon two things, meeting the requirements of our customers, which was achieving ISO-9000 status, and plant efficiency improvement.

After four years of steady training and convincing some diehard, unwilling-to-change senior employees, the company passed its first audit. The audit did not go as planned, and it was discovered that some areas within the plant, having been audited by an outside independent auditing group, needed additional changes. But all employees noticed more consistency in the product being made, the result of better documentation and process control instructions.

This first audit created a change of culture within the company. After operators started documenting what was necessary to perform their processes correctly, they asked for more information and direction. This allowed them to notice that they had a better grasp of what they were producing.

This in turn inspired a tidal wave of improvements within the company and helped improve the company's bottom line. This also led to the balance of personnel, who were not convinced prior to the first audit, coming to believe in the new system.

Training has many purposes, and if done correctly it may help motivate employees, improve efficiencies, allow open positions to be filled from within the company, and much more. In our case, training proved its own importance. Superior training prevents errors and permits workers to produce high-quality products. Poor training generates fires to put out, sometimes when there is little time.

As a manager, though, sometimes it takes a lot of long-term persistence in order to accomplish the end goal. Managers need long-term vision.

CHAPTER 9
ASSESSMENT

1. **What is the difference between quality training and the quality of training?** Most organizations are concerned with the quality of training, and for sound reasons, but quality training is just as essential. One goal that most businesses have is to improve the quality of a product or service.

2. **How does quality training go beyond training?** Quality training helps motivate employees, improve efficiencies, and allows open positions to be filled from within an organization.

CHAPTER CHALLENGE

Choose and write about a business where quality training is emphasized beyond basic training.

10

INNOVATION

> *One of the symptoms of an absence of innovation is the fact that you lose your jobs. Everyone else catches up with you. They can do what you do better than you or cheaper than you. And in a multinational corporate-free market enterprise, it is the company's obligation to take the factory to a place where they can make it more cheaply.* — Neil deGrasse Tyson

CHAPTER PREVIEW

1

There may be a difference between two equally matched companies.

2

Companies need to survive.

3

Innovation keeps people together.

I once received a new bicycle as a Christmas gift. To me, that bike was like a Rolls-Royce. Unfortunately, it was stolen within a year, which broke my heart. I knew that I could wish all I wanted, but that bike was not coming back, so I had to innovate and make a bike out of parts that I could beg, borrow, or steal.

I found a frame, which I painted fire engine red. Then I took a bunch of other random parts (handlebars, wheels, fenders) and polished them so that they shone like a new brass trumpet. My bike was a design that could not be found in any bicycle store. I was so proud of my one-of-a-kind bike. It looked new with the custom paint job, and I saw that with all of my efforts I was able to create something fabulous and ultimately had a bike to ride again.

Business is similar to that bike. Companies may appear to be similar in nature, so what makes one company different from other similar companies? It could be how each business innovates to keep its edge over the competition.

Southwest Airlines was quite innovative when it implemented its no-assigned-seating strategy. This change was a major break from traditional seating practices. It seemed to be a risky move with little perceived value, but it saved time and money. This change made finding seats for customers more efficient. The risk was worth it.[62]

Southwest also did not allow travel agents to sell Southwest airline tickets, so tickets were available only to people who contacted Southwest directly, again a risky and innovative move that improved Southwest's position within the airline industry as a whole.[114]

Innovation is brought about by:

1. The necessity to solve well-defined problems.

2. The changing of direction of an organization.

3. Curiosity to find something of interest.

4. The desire to make profits.

5. The thrill of achieving something or accomplishing an extravagant goal.[71]

Innovation should become a manager's tool. It is a reason to get people together to focus on one goal, need, or topic and make improvements for an organization. If done well, all employees will win and feel that they have a stake in the improvements, and the company adds to its bottom line.

> **Innovation should become a manager's tool.**

There may be times when a manager has to solve a problem or face competition for advancement, so inspiration and innovation must come from a different place than the usual day-to-day thinking.

CHAPTER 10
ASSESSMENT

1. **Why is innovation imperative?** Many companies are similar, so companies should focus on what their artistic differences are. Innovation is the spark that separates one company from another.

2. **What are the personal reasons for innovation?** Innovation inspires employees to work hard to solve problems, it may change the direction of an organization, employees are curious to find something new and interesting, it aids in making profits, and employees desire to achieve something or accomplish a goal.

CHAPTER CHALLENGE

Choose and write about one business that has used innovation well in order to survive.

11

EVOLUTION

CHAPTER PREVIEW

1 Nothing remains forever

2 Evolution is goal-induced.

3 Evolution is more than a product.

As a manager, you have been in business for a long time and thus far have prospered, so you feel that you are in control of all the areas that you need to be in control of and are wise to situations around you. But as stated earlier, a manager should never become comfortable! If a seasoned manager becomes complacent, this is when he should begin to worry.

This concern is justified for a couple of reasons, one of which is that a manager should never feel that he is in total control and that everything is running fine. This is dangerous. People may think that the goal is to feel like everything is rosy and have no worries, but in the real world, a manager must have his guard up at all times.

> **We all need to change, grow, and evolve.**

This sounds bad, but it is reality and a part of the job.

The second part of a seasoned manager's job is to be aware of evolution. After experiencing most or all of the management scenarios detailed in the previous chapters, a manager must use wisdom in order to know what to watch for, but one thing that sneaks up on companies is time.

Products, services, and customers all change over time, so companies must evolve periodically. ABC Engineering Company has luckily gone through numerous evolutions over the last eighty years:

1. The company started in tool and die work, making tools, stamping dies, fixtures, and so on, for other companies.

2. During World War II, it made aerospace parts.

3. After World War II, ABC shifted its main business from aerospace to producing heavy-duty transmission components.

4. In the 1960s, it drifted a bit to making spoke wheels for Schwinn Bicycles, making fluid filling machines, and inventing a small clutch used on machining lathes.

5. By the end of the 1960s, most of the previous products were phased out for a variety of reasons, but then the company entered a new era of making earthmoving components.

6. This lasted through the 1980s, at which time a new product was launched, a special low-weight forming process to fashion splined housing for transmissions and brake assemblies.

7. Through the 1990s, the splined housing business grew to record sales.

8. Now in the 2010s, new lines of business are being developed, which include a laser welding and cutting process and a special heat-treat operation.

Each of these evolutions was conceived with the goal of enhancing previous production while growing into new markets. If the above progressions had not taken place, the company would have gone out of business, as some products that it used to make are no longer in existence.

This is why a manager, especially at upper levels, should not rest or feel comfortable. We all need to change, grow, and evolve.

William Lundin, who passed away in 2000, was a board-certified clinical psychologist, and his wife Kathleen has a background in journalism. Together they analyzed working environments through workshops, training courses, and a collection of books and articles.

As stated in *The Healing Manager*:

> *Management skills can't be reduced to a wallet-sized reminder card. Knowing how to behave comes from inside the person, when the inside is trusting and optimistic. Becoming a healing manager, recognize the reality of your emotions, take pleasure in the growth of others, and you will be better.*[77]

Products are not the only things that must be kept in evolution mode. Process evolution is perhaps the most dynamic of all. In looking at U.S. history, we see that process evolutions have taken place and have had an affect on the world. The Ford Motor Company's use of the production assembly line is one of the most common models of this kind of dramatic change. The use of robots in production, computer numerical control for more precise dimensional control of machines and processes, and steel products changing to plastic composites all represent process and product evolution. Just as with managers, people and products must continue to evolve in order to grow.[65]

Quality is another evolving aspect of business, as it combines process with management and has been ongoing for hundreds of years. But it was a change in the 1950s that did not take place that shaped one major evolution.

W. Edwards Deming tried to tell executives at U.S. automotive manufacturers General Motors, Ford, and others that they needed to make management and production philosophy changes, but these executives ignored Deming, saying thanks but no thanks, an opinion that they would later regret. Japanese officials soon asked Deming to fly to Japan and help Japan rebound because the Japanese economy was in the pits.[32]

Deming's ideas were focused on changing management, thinking about processes but also about the people performing the processes. During Deming's training programs in Japan, he instituted his Fourteen Points for management. All managers should use these 14 Points, as they cover all aspects of managing personnel. Briefly, they are:

1. Create constant improvement of product and service.

2. Adopt new philosophy for change.

3. Cease dependence on inspection (100 percent).

4. End the practice of buy-for-price-only.

5. Improve production, services methods, and employee and customer needs.

6. Train on the job.

7. Institute leadership to help improve operators and management.

8. Drive out fear.

9. Break down barriers.

10. Eliminate slogans.

11. Eliminate standards (quotas).

12. Remove barriers that do not allow employees to have pride in workmanship.

13. Institute education for self-improvement.

14. Put everyone in the company to work to accomplish transformation.[32]

Years later, some of the same companies that had sent Deming away asked for his assistance. One such company was General Motors. In the 1980s, GM instituted a new program called Target For Excellence (TFE). This program was broken down and audited in business sectors, including: Quality, Costs, Leadership, Technology, and Delivery.[109]

Even though Deming had nothing to do with the TFE program, GM hired Deming during the same time period, so new and old quality ideas were utilized in combination with Deming's philosophies.

One of Deming's purposes was to conduct numerous training sessions. Simultaneously, other programs emerged that combined process and management evolutions. Some of these include:

1. **Total Quality Management:** an approach of getting everyone involved with quality.

2. **Just-in-Time Inventory:** managing inventory saves money and improves quality.

3. **Lean Manufacturing:** use the fewest steps to maintain a business from production, paperwork, and management perspectives to improve output per person.

4. **Six Sigma:** control the whole process with in-depth management/ operator training, including statistics.[65]

5. **ISO-9000:** an international approach to make all quality systems equal and effective. This international group used the U.S. quality standard specification MIL-Q-9858 as its foundation.

6. **QS-9000 and later TS 16949:** the automotive approach to the ISO 9000 but a bit more stringent.

7. **NADCAP:** aerospace version of a process in which management controls are reviewed that also watches the actual process at work.[35]

Each one of the above programs provides an evolution opportunity for management to become more involved with establishing a more reliable process control. The take-away here is that not only are options available, but it is also what management does with them.

This is where a manager must decide what may or may not work for her organization. Most of these programs cost a lot of money to implement, and if a program works, it normally saves money. If a program does not work, however, it costs money and sends a negative attitude through the company as a failure of management.

The above-listed programs are not one single program but a maze of programs put together, such as Enterprise Resource Planning (ERP), which combines systems to reduce redundant activities. The process includes how data is entered, how it is used across different platforms, how it may be used to reduce paperwork, and it builds on a Lean manufacturing system. To invest in ERP, a manager must look across different processes within an organization, which may be costly.

Other businesses have evolved as well. United Parcel Service has revolutionized the shipping industry with ideas about how to ship products faster and more efficiently, finding ways to improve the speed of delivery in the 1980s.[125] Some of the ways that UPS accomplished this include adopting an overnight air delivery program, operating its own aircraft, merging different cultures and constructing a seamless operation called UPS Airlines, and initiating a computerized operations, monitoring, planning, and scheduling system called COMPASS.[125]

McDonalds unveils new products on a regular basis to keep customers interested in coming back and to determine which products sell and do not sell. Recently, it released a nutrition-based menu, taking its customers' needs into account.[85]

Target followed Walmart by selling food products in the big-box retail environment.[20] In addition, other companies understand that they cannot stand still and are making similar changes. Look around and you will find some of them.

What does this have to do with managers? Well, managers must see what is around them, but not only within their own organization. Managers must be aware of the competition, current trends, and what customers want in order to make evolution a priority.

CHAPTER 11
ASSESSMENT

1. **What is the difference between innovation and evolution?** Innovation gives a company an opportunity to choose a course of action. Evolution is where a business finds itself going in order to stay in business. Sometimes evolution is not by choice but by necessity.

2. **When may an organization stop evolving?** Never, as Deming so succinctly put it. Improve constantly, or go out of business.

CHAPTER CHALLENGE

Find and write about one business that has used both evolution and innovation in order to survive.

12

SCHEDULING

> *A schedule defends from chaos and whim. It is a net for catching days. It is a scaffolding on which a worker can stand and labor with both hands at sections of time.* — Annie Dillard

CHAPTER PREVIEW

1

Scheduling is not a glorious subject, but it is mandatory.

2

Options are plentiful in relation to scheduling.

3

The times and people cause changes in scheduling methods.

No matter what business a manager is in, a schedule or deadline must be met. There are many different unique ways to schedule depending on the business, but all are used for staying on top of the flow of personnel versus the flow of products or services.

One basic tool that may be utilized is a Gantt chart (Figure 1). It may take on different appearances and uses, but basically it lists one fixed subject and one variable subject, such as personnel with a variety of starting times as opposed to personnel with fixed starting times. A Gantt chart may be used in a restaurant, an automobile workshop, for manufacturing a new product, or construction project timing. For this reason, this type of scheduling chart has endless possible uses.[70]

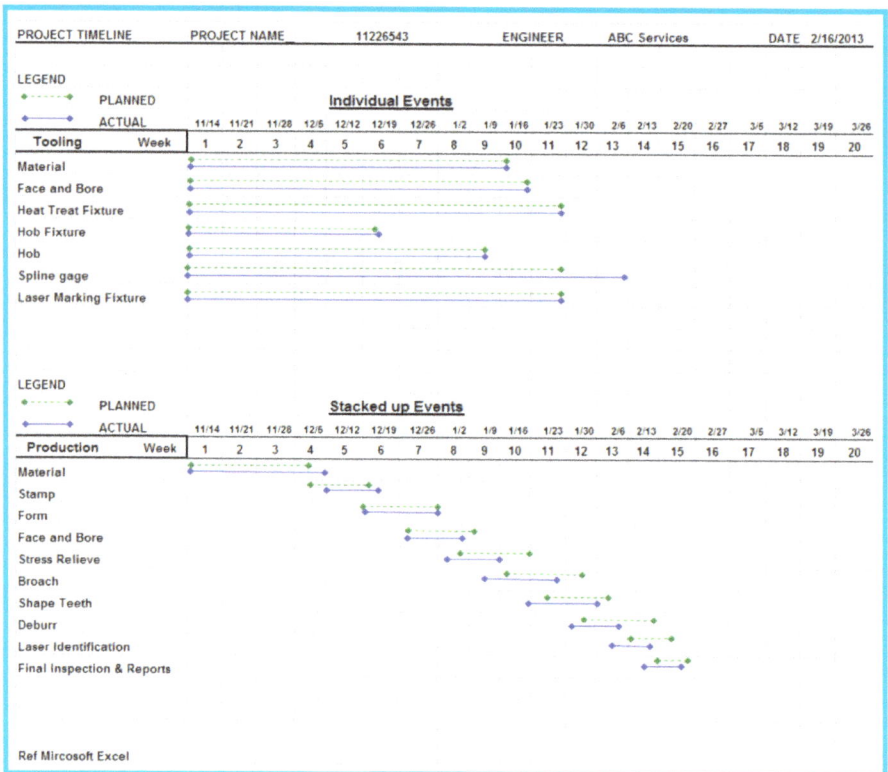

FIGURE 1: GANTT CHART

The chart may be altered depending on scheduling needs at any given time and modified to alert whoever is filling it out to adjust for different circumstances for those time periods.

In the manufacturing environment, employees must report where the machining and other processes are being done, so the schedule must be rigid. This is normally called a fixed schedule. People are needed to run the machines at given times throughout a 24-hour period, so they must be there during these times.

The scheduling is not strict when you have the right number of workers because people may be bounced around to adjust for flow. This happens when training is done correctly and thoroughly. However, this is one area in which manufacturing is presently having difficulties. People want flexibility, and the manufacturing world most times cannot offer it.

The Gantt chart above for manufacturing shows how a new product is conceived by steps and then made. One may feel like a crystal ball is necessary in order to foresee and predict the future.

The top part of the chart shows the schedule for building tools to make steel components. Without this schedule, it would be difficult to know when to plan actual production of parts.

The bottom part of the chart shows the actual process for producing a product and the time necessary to finish each operation, after the tooling depicted in the top part of the chart has been completed. Both sections of this chart are needed to determine if the time frame is acceptable to the customer, which then helps an organization stay on target.

Both parts of the chart are useful, and again, may be used for numerous types of projects. Over time, a Gantt chart becomes an excellent tool for any manager. As you can see, the lower part of the chart above resembles a freight train having many cars that need to go in the same direction.

In some scheduling instances, four ten-hour days in a week may work, if no interference with personnel or machines exist, but this is not a given. Split shifts may also be effective. A split shift may be a school bus driver who works in the morning and returns to work later in the afternoon of the same day. In this case, work schedules may change within the day or the week.

Some schedules may not follow a pattern. In addition, irregular shifts exist, where hours vary, such as with a salesperson. They are not guaranteed forty hours a week or eight-hour days, as every day may be different.[76]

A vastly different type of scheduling is used by EMS and fire departments. A fire department schedule generally averages forty-hour weeks or two hundred and twelve hours over twenty-eight days using twenty-four-hour shifts for each worker.[95] This kind of scheduling also has a three-on, three-off variation of days worked. Police may have similar schedules and work eight- to twelve-hour days. This allows for schedules that rotate through weekend shifts to be fair to everyone in the department.[117]

> ...when people, schedules, and supplies are in the mix, it resembles the aforementioned freight train.

Each type of business has its own method of scheduling, so managers must be aware of all kinds of schedules. The new trend is going toward a more flexible type of scheduling. However, in certain jobs, flexibility is not possible. Even with fixed scheduling, managers must be able to use their imagination. Managers need to know how to address any scheduling conflict.

I have seen scheduling nightmares a number of times in my career. When someone within the system does not show up, not enough people are hired, materials are not available, or the flow of the product is erratic, trouble begins. To get a single process or function going is one thing, but when multiple functions run together, every process must begin and run smoothly.

This sounds easy, but when people, schedules, and supplies are in the mix, it resembles the aforementioned freight train. The first freight car nudges forward, but the rest of the cars do not want to follow. Finally the second car moves, and then the third, but it takes a while before all of the cars get going.

It also takes a lot of extra energy to get this movement started, whether a train or a production schedule, no matter what the business is. The secret is to not let the train slow down to a dead stop. Always keep a process flowing to some degree so that starting up or ramping up to full production will be less dramatic.

In high school, I worked for a fast-food restaurant. Every morning half a crew was scheduled, and then in the early afternoon the full crew came in for the evening rush hour. There were times, for various reasons, that the manager did not schedule correctly, personnel did not show up, or a newspaper ad was not taken into consideration.

In whatever case, the people who came to work knew what needed to be done, but they were unable to do it all before the rush, and then suddenly they were overwhelmed. People were flying everywhere trying to do everything and give the customers what they wanted, and, as expected, the scheduled flow of products to customers was delayed, so customers became irate.

What needed to be done was to *fill the bubble*, which means to find the roadblock and get rid of it. In the above case, another employee should have been called in to work when it became evident to the manager that he was short. That person would have filled the bubble that everyone else tried to fill for the rest of the night.

If you multiply a collapse like this by different departments that need to run with each other, what you get is a ton of inefficient pushing and pulling, which then becomes emotional to those involved. A smooth-running schedule yields a lot less stress for everyone.[70]

CHAPTER 12
ASSESSMENT

1. **Why are some schedules fixed?** In industries such as mining or manufacturing, machines may not be moved around, so the employee must go to where the work is.

2. **Why does scheduling matter?** Having an excess of people on the job wastes money, and if too few people show up for work, the customer will not be happy with poor or slow service.

3. **Why does the author mention the freight train?** This is the perfect analogy for what it takes to get a product or service going. After the flow or service is up and running, it is far easier to keep it moving.

CHAPTER CHALLENGE

Choose and write about a company that has either a poor or a fantastic scheduling program, where you might have seen the freight train effect or the lack thereof.

13

ORGANIZATIONAL STRUCTURE

Every company has two organizational structures: The formal one is written on the charts; the other is the everyday relationship of the men and women in the organization. — Harold S. Geneen

CHAPTER PREVIEW

1

A manager is like a piece in a jigsaw puzzle.

2

Where do people fit within an organization?

3

An organization needs to understand how it is going to operate and communicate in order to be successful.

Managers must learn where they fit within an organizational structure. To whom do they report? Managers are part of a larger picture. They may not know the total plan, but they should know their place in the organization.

To a new manager, the corporate structure may appear like a puzzle with countless pieces. When the individual starts putting the puzzle together, they do not know where the pieces fit. Certain pieces may appear to be in the correct position or look compatible, but they just don't work together.

Knowing where one fits within the corporate structure sounds easy, but surprisingly, most new managers are poor at finding their place. Confusion and floundering on the part of a new manager are signs that she has not yet learned enough about her organizational structure. On the contrary, a savvy manager will learn quickly where she fits within the overall corporate structure. Everyone has a place, and new managers must understand how information flows up and down the organizational ladder.

A prime example of this learning exercise is when a young boy receives his first model airplane. He opens the box and knows that after everything is put together correctly, he will have something that matches the picture on the box. But he doesn't see it initially. There seems to be hundreds of pieces and miscellaneous items.

At first, this boy sits and ponders where to begin. Seeing all of the pieces at one time is overwhelming, and nothing gets done right away. After some thought, the child may ask for help, just as a new manager should do with his supervisor. Then the boy studies his conundrum a bit more.

After some time, he works on a seemingly inconsequential sub-assembly, the same way in which a new manager should look at how the organizational chart functions within his company and note where he fits in. The boy soon sees that the directions are making sense, and the order of assembly becomes more visible.

The boy learns that the overall project is actually a series of mini projects, and then the whole assembly falls into place. As with a new manager, after studying his company, the meaning of the organizational chart is soon perceived, but a new manager should also understand the responsibilities of each person at every level of the chart.

Whether a new business or one re-building, it is the same, a company must recognize the responsibility that it has not only to personnel and to the company itself, but it has a responsibility to the community as well. A company must plan for this additional responsibility, so this also means that a new manager must be aware of this layer that is necessarily added to the organizational structure.

The community factor as discussed in Case Study #1 is called social responsibility. Social responsibility adds an element of credibility to a company from the viewpoint of the people who live, work, and associate with the company. To explain social responsibility in more detail we will review Carroll's Global Corporate Social Responsibility Pyramid:

1. **Economic:** must be profitable via global capitalism rules.
2. **Legal:** must obey all laws in line with what is required by stakeholders.
3. **Ethical:** must be ethical in all forms of business and what is expected by the stakeholders.
4. **Philanthropic:** must be a worthy corporate citizen and follow what is desired by the stakeholders.[71]

The first question that an organizational team must ask is, *can we meet expectations, and how are we going to do this*? Then the organization must decide which type of management system it is going to have. Remember, in some cases, systems are also called cultures, which we will review more closely in later chapters.

Based on the culture, the information within the organization will flow differently, and for the organization to flourish, everyone in the company must know how the information flows. The executives of the company must choose the correct culture for the company and the management organizational structure that it plans to have.

A company may start with one of two types of systems, closed or open. The closed system is self-sufficient and is closed to surrounding environments.[71] It is able to feed itself by supplying its own raw material, do its own manufacturing, market its own goods for sale, and then use the product sold to begin the cycle all over again.[65]

The open system is much more common and requires interaction with the environment in order to survive. This system has seven interactive functions that rely on constant feedback. The open system is broken down as a steady flow of information:

1. **Inputs:** material, money, human effort, and information.

2. **Managerial Sub-System** (systems within the overall organization): goal setting; planning; assembling people, materials, and energies; organizing; implementing; and controlling.

3. **Goals and Values (proven worth) Sub-System:** culture, philosophy, overall goals, group goals, and individual goals.

4. **Technical Sub-System:** knowledge, techniques, facilities, and equipment.

5. **Structure Sub-System:** who does what, how does the work flow through the organization, teams of people that make work groups, who has the authority, which direction does the information flow within an organization, and how are procedures followed, as well as general rules.

6. **Psychosocial Sub-System:** human resources, attitudes, perceptions, motivation, group dynamics, leadership, communications, and interpersonal relationships.

7. **Outputs:** loops information from products, services, human satisfaction, organizational survival, growth, and social benefits together to determine if actions and methods are being received as planned.[71]

Like the young boy building a model, a new manager may be overwhelmed with all of the above details, but at some point in his early career, he must understand how an organization operates. The best way to establish a clear picture of how a management system is organized is with a chart. A chart may be constructed in a number of ways, but usual methods involve a series of boxes in which the names of personnel or titles are written that also delineate who reports to whom.[71]

The Organizational Chart (Figure 2) on page 77 reveals four basic elements that may be found in an organization:

1. **Hierarchy of Authority:** This shows the formal lines of communication along which information flows. Information must not go beyond the next person in line upward.

2. **Division of Labor:** This shows the direction that information flows downward and also that the lower the information goes, the more specialized the jobs become.

3. **Spans of Control:** This shows the actual number of people that report to each person above them.

4. **Line and Staff Positions:** On the chart, a solid line represents a person with authority, whereas a person depicted by a dotted line is a staff person with little to no authority, such as a person in a clerical position. Line and staff positions have value in areas such as research, technical advice, and recommendation but no real authority.[71]

Organizational charts should be posted on information boards periodically so that everyone knows who they are supposed to report to, so that order may be kept in the system.

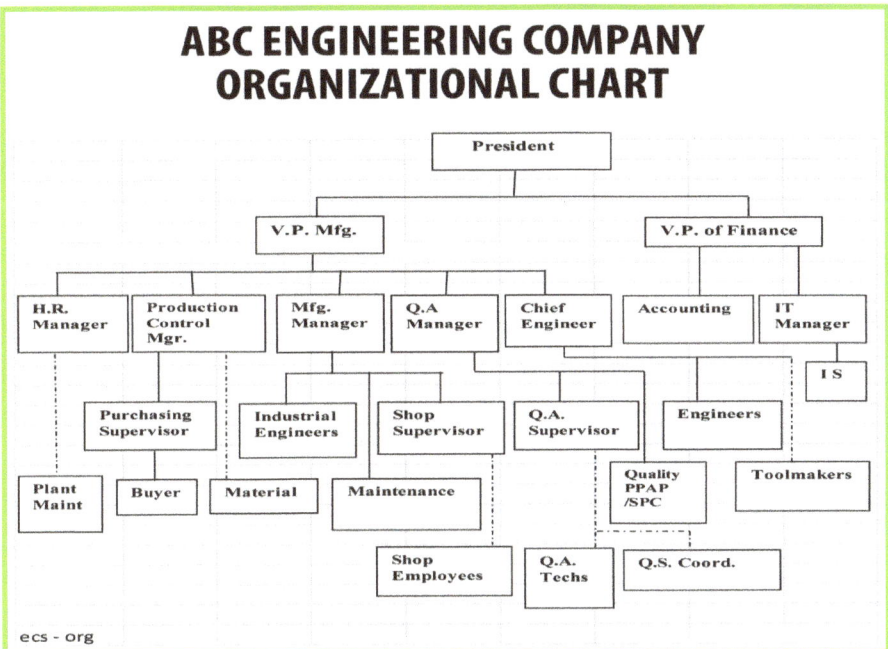

ABC ENGINEERING COMPANY ORGANIZATIONAL CHART

President

V.P. Mfg.

V.P. of Finance

H.R. Manager

Production Control Mgr.

Mfg. Manager

Q.A Manager

Chief Engineer

Accounting

IT Manager

I S

Purchasing Supervisor

Industrial Engineers

Shop Supervisor

Q.A. Supervisor

Engineers

Plant Maint

Buyer

Material

Maintenance

Quality PPAP /SPC

Toolmakers

Shop Employees

Q.A. Techs

Q.S. Coord.

ecs - org

FIGURE 2:ORGANIZATIONALCHART

However, as with most systems, there may be exceptions. One case in point that may prevent conflicts from becoming unmanageable is when an employee reports a problem via the proper channels and nothing is done to correct the problem. There must be a person that everyone in the organization may talk to without fear of retaliation. This person is normally the HR manager, but it does not always have to be. In some cases a district or plant manager may work.

After an organization is established as executives have determined it needs to be, measures should be put into place to verify the effectiveness of the system. One such measure is a system called *Four Ways to Assess Organizational Effectiveness*, developed by K. Camerson. This system takes four individual topics and overlays them so that they are all connected; yet they stay individual (Figure 3).

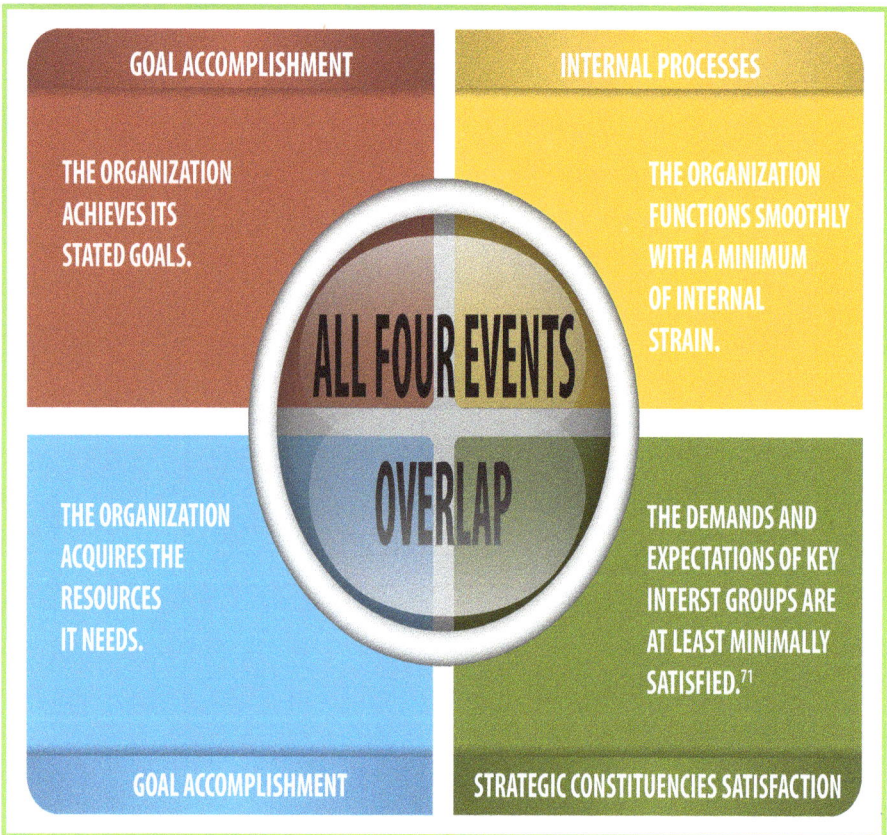

GOAL ACCOMPLISHMENT

THE ORGANIZATION ACHIEVES ITS STATED GOALS.

INTERNAL PROCESSES

THE ORGANIZATION FUNCTIONS SMOOTHLY WITH A MINIMUM OF INTERNAL STRAIN.

ALL FOUR EVENTS OVERLAP

THE ORGANIZATION ACQUIRES THE RESOURCES IT NEEDS.

THE DEMANDS AND EXPECTATIONS OF KEY INTERST GROUPS ARE AT LEAST MINIMALLY SATISFIED.[71]

GOAL ACCOMPLISHMENT

STRATEGIC CONSTITUENCIES SATISFACTION

FIGURE 3: FOUR WAYS TO ASSESS ORGANIZATIONAL EFFECTIVENESS

If the feedback from the application of this test is affirming, it gives the organization a reason to feel that it is functioning properly. This does not mean that other checks and balances should not be put into place, as more ongoing measures provide additional assurance.

While management would be looking for positive results using the above, other signs may show negative results. As stated by R. Kreitner, these possible negative results, *Early Warning Signs of Decline*, are listed in fourteen points:

1. Excess personnel.

2. Tolerance of incompetence.

3. Cumbersome administrative procedures.

4. Disproportionate staff power (technical staff overpowers line managers because the technical staff views managers as too conventional).

5. Replacement of substance with form (planning process becomes more important than results achieved).

6. Scarcity of clear goals and decision benchmarks.

7. Fear of embarrassment and conflict (past manager may resist new ideas for fear of revealing past errors).

8. Loss of effective communication.

9. Outdated organizational structure.

10. Increased scapegoating by leaders.

11. Resistance to change.

12. Low morale.

13. Special interest groups are more vocal.

14. Decreased innovation.[71]

With all factors considered, a management team may avoid total chaos before it happens. However, at some point, change will be required. Change is something that few people look forward to, but it is needed on a regular basis. The more that changes take place, the more comfortable people

> ❝ **The more that change takes place, the more comfortable people become making changes.** ❞

become making changes. The change does not need to be earth-shattering, but the fact that it is a change will continue to build the system toward the future.

All organization strategic plans need to change at some point, as stated by D.R. Fuqua and D.J. Kurpius in their *Conceptual Models in Organizational Consultation*. This model was broken down into categories that link together, which would work in a wide range of different environments:

1. **Inputs:** mission, vision, internal strengths and weaknesses, external opportunities and threats.

2. **Strategic Plans:** strategies and goals.

3. **Target Elements of Change:**

   A. **Organizational Arrangements:** policies, procedures, roles, structure, rewards, settings.

   B. **People:** knowledge, ability, attitude, motivation, behavior.

   C. **Methods:** processes, work flow, job design, technology.

   D. **Social Factors:** organization culture, group processes, interpersonal interaction, communication, leadership.

   E. **Outputs:** organizational level, department/group level, individual level.[71]

As may be seen, the individual items listed are generic, but how they all link together from top to bottom is the pertinent point here. Managers at all levels must understand how the company is structured so that they may work toward achieving the wants and needs of the organization, know how to get promoted, promote employees that will help them and the company's future, and prevent communication errors. Achievement of all of the above points is possible if the organizational structure is comprehensible by all employees.

If a mission or vision is not perceptible to begin with, change will not occur. It is like building a bridge, in that there must be a firm structure at the top and a solid foundation at the bottom with durable links between them holding it all together.

CHAPTER 13 ASSESSMENT

1. **What are the four social responsibilities of a business?** Economic, Legal, Ethical, Philanthropic

2. **What are the methods utilized in an open system of information flow?** Inputs, Managerial Sub-System, Goals and Values Sub-System, Technical Sub-System, Structure Sub-System, Psychosocial Sub-System, Outputs

3. **An organizational chart is broken down into what four elements?** Hierarchy of Authority, Division of Labor, Spans of Control, and Line and Staff Positions

4. **The fourteen points listed above show what?** A warning sign of decline. What to look for and adjust too to prevent total failure.

CHAPTER CHALLENGE

Choose and write about a business whose organizational structure makes sense to you, and detail why it works.

14

RESPECT IS NECESSARY

> *I believe that working with good people matters because then the work environment is good. If there is a sense of respect and belief among the people you work with, that is when good work is done.* — Ranbir Kapoor

CHAPTER PREVIEW

1
In this day and age of instant gratification, respect is not earned immediately.

2
Role-modeling helps.

3
Society is a factor.

You are who you are, do not forget that, but that does not give you the right to treat other people shabbily. The privilege that I found in being poor was that I got to experience the pain of people being mean to me, whether on purpose or because of a lack of understanding. Sometimes this pain was caused unintentionally, while other times it was planned to hurt me and cut into my spirit.

As mentioned earlier, it did not take long as a grade school student for me to see that some parents did not want their children associating with me. At the time, I did not grasp why. Some people found me unacceptable because I was the son of a single mother, and they did not hide their feelings.

Now, how can this be turned into a management lesson? As Joel Osteen says in his book, *I Declare*:

> *People have a right to say what they want, to do what they want... We have a right to overlook it. But when we get upset and go around angry, we change... What they say about you does not determine who you are. Their opinion of you does not determine your self-worth.*[102]

If you are a manager, everyone will have an opinion of you, and you will not be able to please everyone, but this does not give you the right to act like a jackass. Remember, showing respect goes a long way toward pleasing others.

When I was in high school, I thought that I earned respect by being straightforward and honest. I found out soon enough that respect was not a short-term proposition. At my high school graduation, some students told me to get lost, I did not belong with their kind of people. I discovered then that earning respect took a long time.

As a manager, though you cannot please everyone, you must treat others with respect if you wish to receive it in return. However, a fine line exists when people are involved.

I have worked with some tough people with whom others could not get along. I found out that by stopping to listen to their complaints or ideas, and then reacting to their comments and wishes as much as I could, they in turn gave me information, suggestions, and opportunities that I would have missed, and this continues even now. All comments made were not favorable, but I did not get angry, so believe it or not, everybody won.

Some managers may not understand why they cannot communicate with bullies, but in reality

> **...though you cannot please everyone, you must treat others with respect if you wish to receive it in return.**

it is not rocket science. The answer is to show everyone respect and to take action. Did this happen in my first years as a manager? No, it did not. People do not forget where others come from, and in my case, I came up through the ranks, so at each step I had to prove myself all over again.

I accepted that. I recalled the lesson that I had learned at my high school graduation, where I thought that I had earned the respect of others but instead was asked to leave because I was not like them. I then realized that people do not forget where you come from and that it takes a long time to convince people that you are the real deal.

One method by which to show employees what respect looks like is to role-play as part of training. When a person must act as if she is on the receiving end of disrespect, she tends to see the interaction in a different light.

William and Kathleen Lundin conducted training sessions, presented in *The Healing Manager*, which illustrated different situations and how role-playing allowed all parties to see how it felt to be on the wrong side of a conflict. Some of the sub-titles used by the Lundins explain the conditions that they focused on that may exist in the workplace:

1. Employees Are Treated Like Foster Children

2. If You Could Whisper One Thing

3. People Before Process

4. We Live in an Angry Society

5. A Supervisor with Low Self-Esteem

6. Exercise for Trust[77]

These classroom activities engendered an atmosphere of respect between the participants so that discord could be understood before things got out of hand. Again, it seems so simple, but more than any other problem, I have seen numerous managers not handle well the subject of respect. It may be difficult because sometimes things are not black and white, but a manager must learn to always treat others with respect.

When a manager feels that people are responding to her, she is doing it right. Treating everyone with respect will pay you big dividends.

CHAPTER 14
ASSESSMENT

1. **Everyone wants things now, but why does respect take time?** Trust is built with consistent actions across time, and with trust respect may be earned.

2. **What conditions should a manager keep in mind that may aid her in fostering respect, as suggested by the Lundins?** Employees Are Treated Like Foster Children, If You Could Whisper One Thing, People Before Process, We Live In An Angry Society, A Supervisor With Low Self-Esteem, Exercise For Trust.

CHAPTER CHALLENGE

Recall and write about a personal story of when it took you some time to earn respect.

15

HONESTY

Ethics or simple honesty is the building blocks upon which our whole society is based, and business is a part of our society, and it's integral to the practice of being able to conduct business, that you have a set of honest standards. — Kerry Stokes

CHAPTER PREVIEW

1 It is not always easy to be honest.

2 Honesty is not always profitable.

3 Lack of honesty creates a corrupt environment.

In my early teens, my family's income was well below the poverty line, and money was not easy to come by. I lived in a four-apartment building in one apartment with less than 600 square feet, furnished with cheap, decrepit furniture. We did not have a car, and on plenty of occasions I wore the same clothes to school two days in a row because I had a limited number of nice clothes. I had to wash them by hand.

Then one day, I did a stupid thing. I shoplifted food. This was inexcusable and dead wrong. I had to pay the price and go to court. Because it was my first offense, the judge gave me a break, but to be honest, it was not the fear of the judge that caused my greatest pain. It was what I did to my mother. I hurt her dearly. To her, I was no longer the honest son, and I knew it.

I was never dishonest again. This proved to be another lesson in my life and in my rise through the ranks to management.

I see no excusable reason to be dishonest. Yes, as a manager, you may run across information that cannot be given to all employees because of the nature of business. But I am referring to blatant lies to employees to avoid conflict or to advance in management. Lying is a bad habit, and once it is done the first time, that habit may be hard to break.

> **Honesty is at the heart of respect. Moreover, it prevents additional management problems from manifesting.**

Honesty is at the heart of respect. Moreover, it prevents additional management problems from manifesting.

Business finance is a critical function of any organization. This does not mean that the personnel side of business is less valid. But with scandals involving Enron and WorldCom, the terms ethics and finance have become inverse functions of each other and the subject of scrutiny, publicity, and legal actions, all because of uncontrolled greed or the unquestioning following of orders delivered by managers.[141,130]

In a recent case in Milwaukee, Wisconsin, Koss Industries' Vice President of Finance, Sujata Sachdeva, was charged with and found guilty of embezzlement of more than $30 million dollars from the company for personal gain.[130] Sachdeva embezzled the funds by shifting money via wire transfers, checks, and petty cash, but this was not accomplished alone. Her assistant, Julie Mulvaney, aided her.[130] This is why checks and balances related to all monetary activities in any organization should be put into place.

In this case, management could not be trusted, and employees were expected to perform unethical actions. This speaks poorly of the company as a whole and sends the wrong message to all other employees. The way to salvage the reputation of the company was with aggressive action, which meant that Ms. Sachdeva was charged in federal court.

Dishonesty is not limited to finance, it can happen anywhere in a business. Even though it may not be apparent, managers face a lot of pressure at all levels. When a manager fixes production numbers, for instance, he must continue, and when an organization accepts this kind of dishonesty, it becomes the nature of the business. Control must be exerted from the top down as well as from the bottom up.

CHAPTER 15
ASSESSMENT

1. **One of the most talked about problems in management is how people try to cheat the system to get ahead, in one way or another. This is true, and it still takes place. Managers need to think about what, that is necessary for everyone to feel accepted and valued?** Respect, honor, and honesty all go hand-in-hand. A manager cannot have one without the others. If a manager cannot foster an environment of honesty and respect, then he or she should not be a manager.

2. **To be a competent manager, a person must have what?** Honesty, morals, and scruples

CHAPTER CHALLENGE

Find and write about a company or a person who has displayed honesty and/or that has shown that honesty, honor, respect, and morals go hand-in-hand.

16

STORIES OF DISHONESTY

People want to work with somebody who feels shame, who worries about the perceptions of others. Dishonesty is something we don't like in others. — Frans de Waal

CHAPTER PREVIEW

1
Dishonesty may be caused by greed.

2
Dishonesty is a bad habit.

3
People know who is dishonest.

In the retail business, some managers have friends buy products on one day and then return them later, normally after the end of a month or an accounting period. This inflates the store's sales figures for a certain period of time.

Similarly, in manufacturing, when scrap is made in a production process (forming, machining, grinding), scrap material may not be turned in, so it does not show up as a negative cost figure for that department. These kinds of misrepresentations may initially be insignificant, but after the first occurrence, the manager is forced to come up with some way to cover up previous lies. When a manager supervises in this style, it generates poor attitudes and may breed additional dishonesty in employees, so everyone loses.

> **Co-workers are astute, and it does not take long before the truth is known by all.**

Another type of dishonesty, which is not as apparent but is still a morale breaker, is when an employee comes up with an idea that helps an organization to improve costs or working conditions, and the manager claims full credit for the idea.

I once worked with an engineer, who was known to be lazy, but who ostensibly came up with suggestions to improve production. However, I had been warned by other employees that his suggestions were normally not his own, so I decided to test this theory one day.

I had an idea about how to better assemble several metal components during a manufacturing operation, so I showed the idea to this engineer, and he jotted down some notes. Later that month, I asked the chief engineer if he had heard the idea to better assemble the metal components. He said that his engineer had come up with an idea to help, so I asked if I could see the idea, and sure enough, it was my idea.[35]

I let it go at that, chalking it up to another learning experience. But I never gave this engineer any additional concepts or designs and thereafter watched to see how others responded to this dishonest practice. It did not take long before I saw that others refrained from giving this engineer suggestions as well, so his effectiveness definitely suffered over time. But so did the company, as employees then needed to find other managers to whom to give their concepts. If employees do not find an outlet for their ideas, their ideas die.

Another example of a poor choice made by some managers is making information appear different than it actually is. I witnessed this recently when a manager explained in a meeting that he had decided to have a new individual begin work at different times on different days in order to help the company cover two different shifts.

Based on past practices, it was not common for this area and this manager to have employees begin work at various times. The individual in question made it through a probationary period and was hired by the company as a full-time employee.

Within one year, this employee was terminated for poor attendance. The manager had been covering for the employee's absences by revising the schedule at later dates.

If the manager had been honest and up-front, he would have avoided losing a lot of time making changes in his schedule when this person did not show up for work. In addition, a substantial amount of time was lost in disciplining the employee, which led to his termination. This manager was not disciplined, due to a lack of evidence, but his supervisors never trusted him again.

Honesty is undervalued, but it is the foundation upon which trust and reputation are built, and it allows all employees at all levels to have self-esteem.[65]

Honesty is a two-way street. Trust must be built between honest employees and honest managers. It should come as no surprise that both employees and managers see what is happening, no matter how well people try to hide things. Co-workers are astute, and it does not take long before everyone knows the truth.

In later chapters, we will discuss the law, which is another incentive to remain honest. People may forget that it takes a second to lose a reputation that took years to build.

CHAPTER 16
ASSESSMENT

1. **What is one of the best ways for a manager to save time?** Don't cheat and lie. It takes more time to make up numbers or reasons for inconsistencies than it does to tell the truth.

2. **Do managers really get away with being dishonest?** Managers think they do, but co-workers are astute and see more than managers think they do.

CHAPTER CHALLENGE

Find and write about a company or a person for whom it paid to be honest.

17

PEOPLE: THE RIGHT CHOICE

In order to cultivate a set of leaders with legitimacy in the eyes of the citizenry, it is necessary that the path to leadership be visibly open to talented and qualified individuals of every race and ethnicity. — Sandra Day O'Connor

CHAPTER PREVIEW

1	2	3
There are ways to find and choose the right people.	Establish a building-block program.	Sometimes your initial choice must be reversed.

When I was 10 years old, I knew a lot of kids within a mile radius of my house, some of whom could not be trusted, but one person I knew that I could trust was a boy named Paul. We both had the same interest in sports and music, and I saw that he obeyed the rules that his parents put in place. Paul listened to and followed the directions that his parents gave him, which most other kids his age did not do. He showed me that it was easier to follow directions than to make excuses. This is the kind of person whom you want on your work team.

Right before high school, Paul transferred to a private school, so we parted ways. I then became friends with another neighbor named Peter. Peter was also an honest, straightforward person. His parents came to the United States from Germany, and both were hard-working people. I could see that even in my early teens.

Peter's parents showed me and taught me, with few words, that life in the United States was much more blessed with opportunities than their home country at that time. Choices like where to go to school (especially college), where to work, and even where to live were more plentiful in the U.S. On cold days, they even took me to school; otherwise, I would have had to walk three miles.

> **Finding qualified people does not end with placing them in their first position.**

Peter and his family taught me that hard-working people are all around us, but you have to look closely and listen to what people say. People who work hard do not always use many words, but what they lack in volume they make up for in content. A manager wants people like this on her team.

A manager must look at personalities, mannerisms, conduct,

ethics, and much more to place the right person in the correct position. Some traits are hard to discern during an interview, such as how someone might follow the rules and how hard they will work, but others may be discovered in the time in which an interview takes place.

Tests, surveys, and other means are available to help managers narrow down the choices; however, the decision may often come down to a gut feeling. In most cases, if a seasoned manager has a bad feeling, it is normally justified.

To ensure the optimal choice, more than one manager should be involved in the interviewing process, as one manager may miss something that another manager picks up on during the interview, because it is easier for one person to listen while others are talking.

One guide to thin out a number of people is to review whether each person:

1. Builds relationships.

2. Uses integration thinking.

3. Drives toward results.

4. Leads in a learning environment.

5. Takes personal ownership.[88]

This list is primarily used when promoting from within an organization, as several people would have had the chance to see whether candidates exemplify the attributes on the list. However, this list may also be used when interviewing a new person, if a manager so desired and felt that she was astute enough to sift through any answers given.

Finding qualified people does not end with placing them in their first position. When someone is promoted, the process of picking the right person to replace him or her begins anew. As stated above, a series of tests, surveys, and trials are available to help managers limit the choices, but again, a manager's gut feeling is necessary.

Another cause for concern that some managers over look is called The Peter Principle, a concept developed by Dr. Laurence J. Peter and Raymond Hull, in which a person is promoted past their competency level.[23] This frequently happens after someone shows abilities at a position to which they were previously promoted, which does not mean that this person will thrive at a higher-level position.

When reviewing personnel, a manager should view all candidates as if no previous information is known concerning that individual. This may seem like overkill and a time-consuming endeavor, but the alternative may be far worse.

If someone is promoted beyond his skill level, unpleasant consequences may occur. First, others working with this new leader may notice the lackluster abilities. The employees reporting to this person may feel worthless because it becomes apparent that this manager is going nowhere, and the employees will have few chances to feel valued.

The effects of a badly promoted manager on employees may cause entire areas to suffer by means of poor performance and missed quotas, among other things. Second, a manager may notice co-worker animosity, as others may feel that they should have been promoted into that position instead and that they proved their worth but were overlooked. These individuals will not help the struggling leader, which, again, may cause a department to fail.

If a promotion to manager is not working, this person must be demoted or let go. This is why, before promoting someone, a manager should take extra steps, even with existing personnel, to prevent having to take negative actions later. Demotion, if done correctly, may work, as it will solve the problem of lack of performance, but it will also salvage the career of the person placed in the wrong position by making them effective again.

Remember, keeping a person in the wrong position does not solve anything, so to recover from this mistake, the company must be able to assist the individual with keeping his dignity intact because one's reputation means everything. People have feelings, and as a manager, you must determine if the person in the wrong position still has worth. If so, put them where they will best serve the company, but also make the transition work for the individual.

CHAPTER 17
ASSESSMENT

1. **The foundation for future managerial promotions is based on one express factor, which is?** A manager must make the right choice when promoting someone and also in replacing the person promoted so that they may then move up as well.

2. **What are the effects of a badly promoted manager on other employees?** Entire areas may suffer because of poor performance and missed quotas. A manager may notice co-worker animosity, as others may feel that they were overlooked and should have been promoted instead. These individuals will not help the struggling leader, which may cause a department to fail.

CHAPTER CHALLENGE

Find and write about a company that demonstrates the ability to find and promote the right people to the right positions.

18

TEAMS

Teamwork is the ability to work together toward a common vision. The ability to direct individual accomplishments toward organizational objectives. It is the fuel that allows common people to attain uncommon results. — Andrew Carnegie

CHAPTER PREVIEW

1

Choosing the right person is more important when teams are involved.

2

Teams are meant to enhance the work environment.

3

Teams may use a variety of methods to stay on track.

I will digress here for a moment. Back in grade school during recess and gym class, kids used a selection process that brought light to team-building, although, of course, at that age team-building was the furthest thing from anyone's mind. The process involved picking teams for baseball, football, basketball, and other team sports.

Normally, the teacher chose two gifted athletes; in this case, we will call them seasoned managers. The two leaders each selected a player, and perhaps bargained back and forth, until all players were picked. This process, as basic as it is, today serves several purposes:

1. It makes individuals try harder. They do not want to be the weakest member of the team or the last person picked.

2. It forces the leaders to carefully analyze each player for skills and abilities that would be useful in the sport at hand.

3. It ultimately allows for diversity by combining the abilities of all team members.

4. Team members learn that teamwork is all about sharing responsibility.

5. Team members discover that teamwork takes practice.

6. An exceptional leader teaches that teamwork is both a noun and a verb.

7. A manager helps members of his team see that teamwork is an individual skill.[126]

8. The rate of return per individual declines in groups of five or more. Teams may monitor themselves more efficiently than managers do.[64]

Does the above still sound like a reasonable method for choosing teams? Yes. Teams have been picked this way over the years, and the worst thing that ever happened was that one team lost the game. However, today, more is at stake.

In my early grade school years, I was one of those players picked last, but by the end of grade school, I was near the first one selected. I accepted the challenge as an individual to work harder to get better at the game being played. The same is true in employment situations.

Ken Blanchard and Paul Hersey are known internationally for their four different situational leadership models.[11]

In his article *Situational Leadership*, published in *Leadership Excellence* in May 2008, Mr. Blanchard states that a seasoned manager with experience will have already learned about certain qualities that a leader must have:

1. Directing with structure, control, and supervision.

2. Supporting with praise, listening, facilitating, and creating enthusiasm.

3. Coaching by setting goals, developing action plans, and making decisions while maintaining low support.

4. Delegating activities by relinquishing some day-to-day decision making.[10]

Whether choosing students or employees who are trying to improve, managers must put together teams to tackle projects and goals. As a student with weak athletic skills, I would not have learned to improve if I had not received direction, support, and praise from teachers who showed me that setting goals, self-awareness, and hard work would be needed.

Managers need to assess all people who are available for any given position and the attributes that they bring to the job. Managers should look for offensive and defensive team members who can play as one single group.

This is easier said than done, because human nature is responsible for variable conditions that the group must be able to adjust for, specifically, different person-

> **Make certain that leadership structures individual effort to meet group goals.**

alities. At the same time, a manager wants team members who know what is going on and who have the ability to think about the process, people willing to see things from a variety of perspectives and who want to flourish.

This whole process sounds simple, but it is not. The group must have goals in order to verify that it is staying on track. The chances of success are improved if managers do the following:

1. Have a tangible goal.

2. Make sure that the right people are doing the right tasks.

3. Make certain that leadership structures individual effort to meet group goals.

4. Make sure that all group members commit to group goals.

5. Remember that diversity maybe both positive and negative.[126]

Managers who follow all of the above guidelines and strive to achieve these goals will build victorious teams.

CHAPTER 18
ASSESSMENT

1. **Now that you have picked the correct individuals for your team, how do you get them to get along?** Individuals try harder because they do not want to be the weakest link in a group. The idiosyncrasies of each individual, forces the group leader to carefully analyze everyone's skills and abilities to permit diversity by combining abilities.

2. **How might a team best be successful?** Have a tangible goal. Make sure that the right people are doing the right tasks. Make certain that leadership structures individual efforts to meet group goals. Make sure that all group members commit to group goals. Remember that diversity may be both positive and negative.[1]

CHAPTER CHALLENGE

Choose and write about a team that has triumphed against the odds and determine why or how it triumphed.

PART II

SECOND SEASON

19

PLANTING THE SEED

Pay attention to those employees who respectfully ask why. They are demonstrating an interest in their jobs and exhibiting a curiosity that could eventually translate into leadership ability. — Harvey Mackay

CHAPTER PREVIEW

1 Just like tending a garden, effort put into teaching and mentoring will let you reap greater rewards.

2 Teaching leads to avoidance of costly errors in management.

3 How an individual uses limited information maybe a good indicator of his future.

At 25 years old, I became the youngest supervisor, the first level of management with direct contact with production employees, that my company had ever had. This was a double-edged sword for both the company and for me. I knew nothing about the business but thought that I did. It did not take long to realize that I did not know how to handle people, business finances, labor laws, and more, so I took a crash course in business as a whole. This was not the best method of on-the-job training, as costly errors could have been made.

One of a manager's responsibilities is to give employees who appear to be promotable short training sessions in their present positions, which is known as planting the seed. This provides an employee with a training environment in which she should feel little to no pressure.

> **One of a manager's responsibilities is to give employees who appear to be promotable short training sessions in their present positions, which is known as planting the seed.**

This would be similar to a rookie playing baseball at the Triple-A level, where the players get the chance to learn the sport in a low-pressure environment. This way, when a player is called up to the major leagues, he better understands his job, and the odds of best performance are improved. I was not allowed this privilege.

Whether a company is publicly traded or is held privately, promotable employees should be made aware of how the company works. No trade secrets need be given out, but personnel who have shown interest in progressing in a company need to be privy to some of the sensitive areas of an organization so that they may see how the company makes a profit. After all, without profit, the company does not stay in business. Plus, what the individual does with the limited information will let management know if the person is truly a candidate for promotion.

Labor laws are never-ending and always changing, and this is why managers must be aware of the labor laws affecting the company. Lawsuits are costly to companies. In a number of cases, a costly court battle may be avoided with intervention by a manager, which we will cover later.

As has been seen, there is a significant people side to management, but there are other sides as well, such as presenting information, the law, economics, marketing, global influences, and more, all of which are focused on in Part II of this book.

CHAPTER 19
ASSESSMENT

1. **What are the benefits of planting the seed early?** Both management and the promotable individual get the chance to see what the individual can do and learn before the real pressure is on them. In some cases, both parties find out that the individual does not have what is necessary for promotion.

2. **How much information should a promotable employee be given?** Trade secrets need not be revealed, but those who have shown interest in being promoted should be privy to some of the sensitive areas of the company. Also, providing limited information to certain employees allows management to determine if someone is indeed a candidate for promotion.

CHAPTER CHALLENGE

Choose and write about a case in which planting the seed may be seen in the real business world.

20

PRESENTATIONS

Precision of communication is important, more important than ever, in our era of hair-trigger balances, when a false or misunderstood word may create as much disaster as a sudden thoughtless act. — James Thurber

CHAPTER PREVIEW

1

The first challenge is overcoming fear.

2

A new set of tools is needed to excel at giving presentations.

3

If investigation is weak, the presentation will be as well.

I have seen throughout my years in management that new managers are often weak in the area of putting together and giving presentations. Numerous reasons exist for this, including scant knowledge of computer tools, lack of experience speaking in front of people, and failure to organize group meetings with agendas.

Inevitably, a manager will have to give a presentation at some point. If a manager wants to advance in an organization, she must practice her presentation skills.

I have first-hand knowledge of this truth. As a young manager, I attended a W. Edwards Deming seminar. Little did I know that during the night dining session, we were going to be asked to solve a problem, after dividing up into small groups. The next day one person from each group had to explain, with the use of the new information and tools that we had been given, what the solution was to the problem.

Guess what? My group picked me as the spokesman. This was the first time that I had ever had to give a presentation in front of roughly three hundred people. While standing in front of all of those people, I could feel and see my heart beating through my shirt. But as the saying goes, practice makes perfect. After this experience I forced myself to be prepared for when the next speaking event would arise, and it has, numerous times.

> **Inevitably, a manager will have to give a presentation at some point.**

Figures 4 through 10 are slides from an actual presentation, using Microsoft Power-Point, that explains a Six Sigma program. The presentation was given to the VP of Manufacturing and later to a business class at Cardinal Stritch University.[35] The purpose of each slide is described beneath its image. Presentations may be organized in many ways, but these rules are helpful in all of them:

1. Make sure that the purpose of the presentation is clear in the first one to two slides.

2. Keep the number of words per slide to a minimum. Complete sentences are not necessary.

3. Use pictures and charts to reduce words, but keep them simple, or it becomes confusing.

4. Reiterate the purpose of the presentation in the middle of it.

5. Conclude with a short but pointed reason for the presentation.

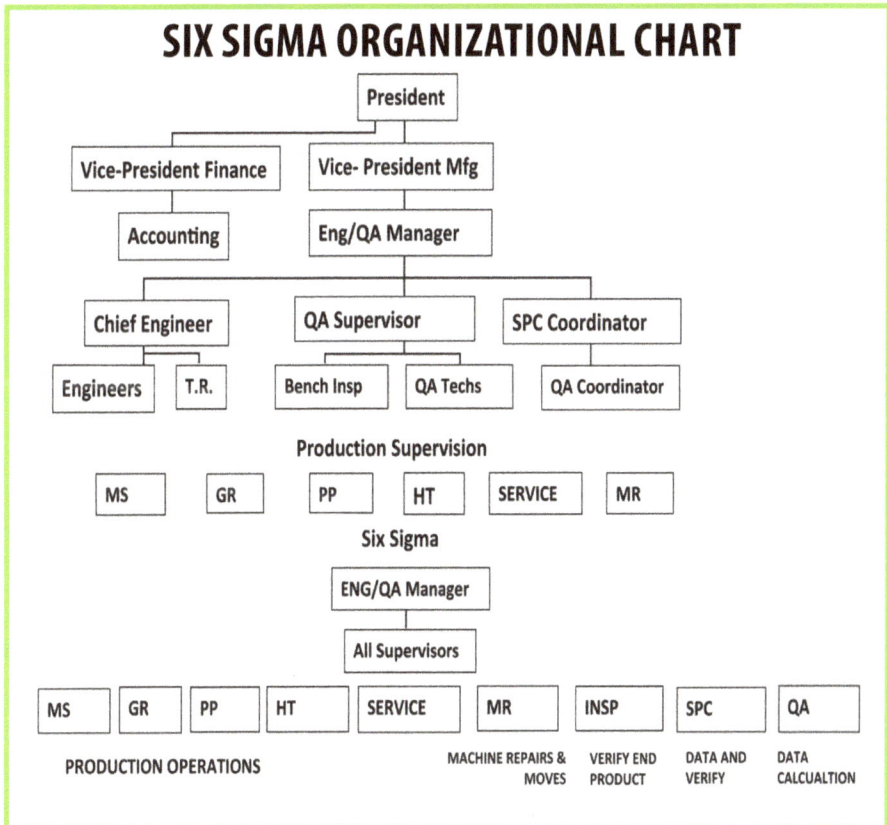

SIX SIGMA ORGANIZATIONAL CHART

President

Vice-President Finance — Vice-President Mfg

Accounting — Eng/QA Manager

Chief Engineer — QA Supervisor — SPC Coordinator

Engineers — T.R. — Bench Insp — QA Techs — QA Coordinator

Production Supervision

MS — GR — PP — HT — SERVICE — MR

Six Sigma

ENG/QA Manager

All Supervisors

MS	GR	PP	HT	SERVICE	MR	INSP	SPC	QA
PRODUCTION OPERATIONS				MACHINE REPAIRS & MOVES	VERIFY END PRODUCT	DATA AND VERIFY	DATA CALCUALTION	

FIGURE 4: EXPLAINS THE CHAIN OF COMMAND FOR THE PROGRAM AND INDICATES SUPPORT FROM THE TOP DOWN

For additional information on presentations, you may wish to review Microsoft Office products.[45] Microsoft PowerPoint is a first-rate program for all managers to learn and use. If it is not needed when a manager first starts out, he will certainly wish at some point that he had studied PowerPoint tools. Presentations may also be a means of expressing a variety of thoughts effectively in a short period of time.

PROCESS COST OPTIONS PROCESS COST OPTIONS

OPTION 1
Grob Cell, Okuma Lathe/JoJo Cell/ Okuma Lathe • JoJo machine time is 31 seconds (one can rotation)

Op#	Description	Notes	Actual Pcs Per Hour	Std Hours	Pay Grade	Base Rate	Cost per Piece
22	Blank OD	timed	392.16	0.2550	4	14.50	$0.0370
51	Draw	timed	83.61	0.0120	5	14.35	0.1716
60	Wash	timed	181.62	0.0055	8	13.82	0.0760
New	CNC Grob #3 / Perf / "U" Form	estimate	30.14	0.0332	5	14.35	0.4761
162	Okuma Face and JoJo Trim, Pierce and Lance	estimate	45.31	0.0221	5	14.35	0.3167
165	Okuma Turn Sensor Band	timed	33.72	0.0297	5	7.18	0.2128
172	Wash	timed	253.81	0.0039	8	13.82	0.0545
175	Vibromill	timed	61.24	0.0163	8	13.82	0.2257
185	Check 100%	timed	34.19	0.0295	9	13.65	0.3993

TOTAL LABOR COST PER PIECE: $1.970

OPTION 2
Grob Cell, Okuma Lathe/JoJo Cell/ Okuma Lathe • JoJo machine time is 31 seconds (one can rotation)

Op#	Description	Notes	Actual Pcs Per Hour	Std Hours	Pay Grade	Base Rate	Cost per Piece
22	Blank OD	timed	392.16	0.2550	4	14.50	$0.0370
51	Draw	timed	83.61	0.0120	5	14.35	0.1716
60	Wash	timed	181.62	0.0055	8	13.82	0.0760
New	CNC Grob #3 / Perf / "U" Form	estimate	30.14	0.0332	5	14.35	0.4761
162	Okuma Face and JoJo Trim, Pierce and Lance	estimate	45.31	0.0221	5	14.35	0.5667
172	Wash	timed	253.81	0.0039	8	13.82	0.0545
175	Vibromill	timed	61.24	0.0163	8	13.82	0.2257
185	Check 100%	timed	34.19	0.0295	9	13.65	0.3993

TOTAL LABOR COST PER PIECE: $2.007

OPTION 3
Grob Cell, Okuma Lathe/JoJo Cell/ Okuma Lathe • JoJo machine time is 31 seconds (one can rotation)

Opt#	Description	Notes	Actual Pcs Per Hour	Std Hours	Pay Grade	Base Rate	Cost Per Piece
22	Blank OD	timed	392.16	0.2550	4	14.50	$0.0370
51	Draw	timed	83.61	0.0120	5	14.35	0.1716
60	Wash	timed	181.62	0.0055	8	13.82	0.0760
New	CNC Grob #3 / Perf / "U" Form	estimate	30.14	0.0332	5	14.35	0.4761
115	Okuma Face only	timed	36.39	0.0275	5	7.18	0.1972
New	JoJo Trim, Pierce and Lance	estimate	80.26	0.0125	7	13.97	0.1741
165	Okuma Turn Sensor Band	timed	33.72	0.0297	5	7.18	0.2128
172	Wash	timed	253.81	0.0039	8	13.82	0.0545
175	Vibromill	timed	61.24	0.0163	8	13.82	0.2257
185	Check 100%	timed	34.19	0.0295	9	13.65	0.3993

TOTAL LABOR COST PER PIECE: $2.024

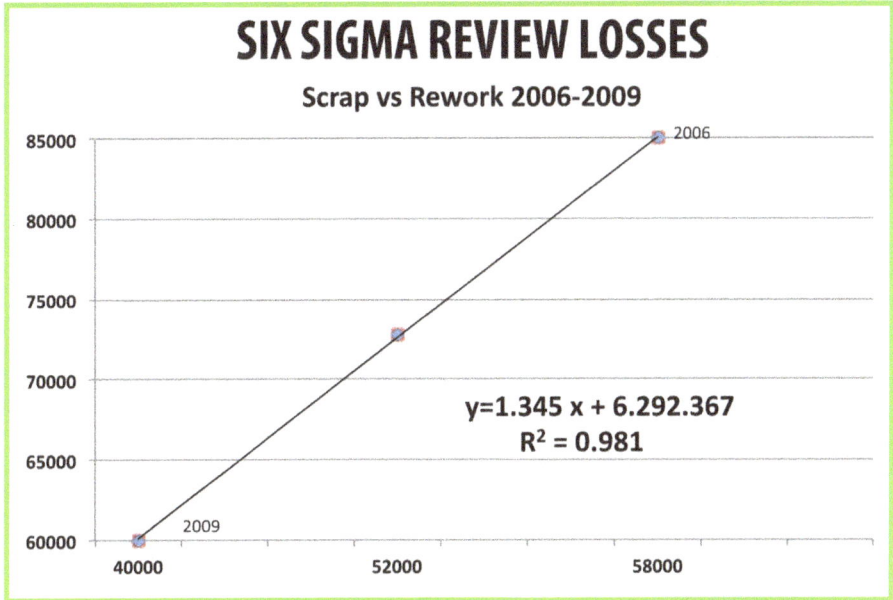

SIX SIGMA REVIEW LOSSES

Scrap vs Rework 2006-2009

$y=1.345 \, x + 6.292.367$
$R^2 = 0.981$

FIGURE 6: ONE MAIN AREA OF COSTS (LOSSES) IS SCRAP AND REWORK. WHICH IS WORSE BY COMPARISON? BOTH LOSSES ARE RELATED, BUT SCRAP NEEDED WORK FIRST.

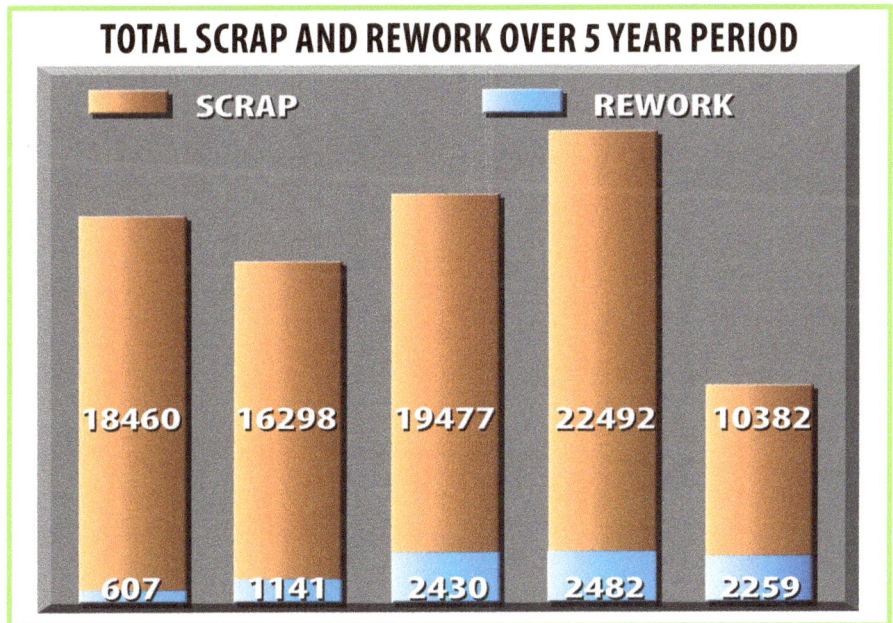

TOTAL SCRAP AND REWORK OVER 5 YEAR PERIOD

SCRAP   REWORK

| 18460 | 16298 | 19477 | 22492 | 10382 |
| 607 | 1141 | 2430 | 2482 | 2259 |

FIGURE 7: THE ACTUAL RESULT OF SCRAP AND REWORK IS SHOWN BY METHODS OF CHARTING, WHICH MAY ALLOW FOR A MORE DYNAMIC PRESENTATION.

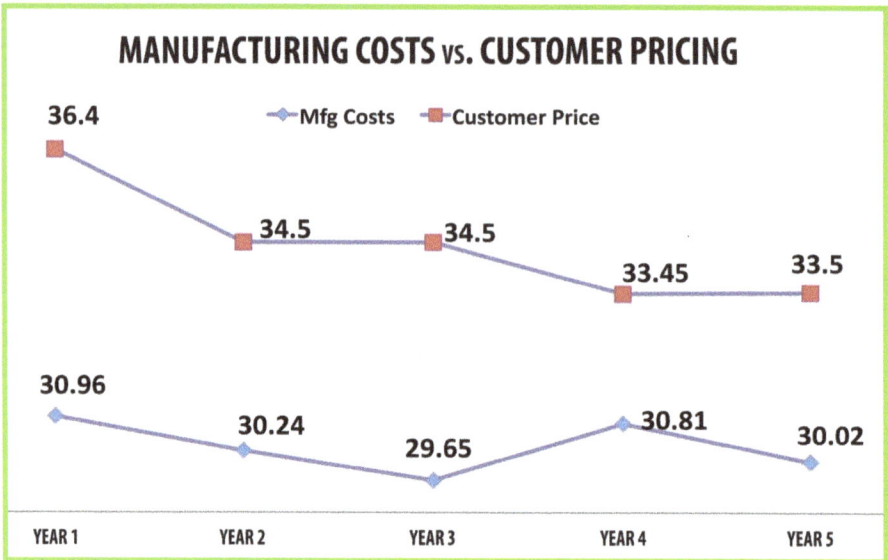

MANUFACTURING COSTS vs. CUSTOMER PRICING

FIGURE 8: THE CUSTOMER'S CONCERN IS ALWAYS PRICE, AND THIS SLIDE SHOWS PRICE REDUCTIONS BUT NO REAL MANUFACTURING COSTS REDUCTIONS, WHICH DOES NOT WORK OVER A LONG PERIOD OF TIME.

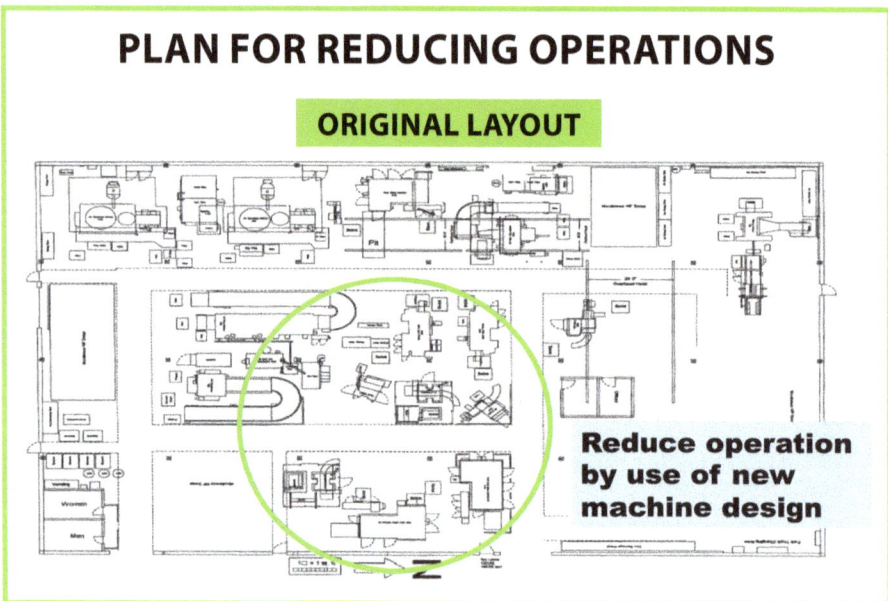

PLAN FOR REDUCING OPERATIONS

ORIGINAL LAYOUT

Reduce operation by use of new machine design

FIGURE 9: THE PLAN WAS TO MAKE A MANUFACTURING CELL AND TO SHOW HOW IT MIGHT LOOK TO ACHIEVE LOWER MANUFACTURING COSTS.

Six Sigma Does Not End

III. 2010 goal and savings initiatives. 5 direct and 5 nondirect savings

   A.   Direct savings would be

      1. See submitted price reduction proposal on Part Number 345421 and 346543 in which we are awaiting your response to this significant cost savings

      2. Flexplate spotwelding kits. One part number and an assembly savings at Company Z

      3. Buffed surface wearplates. Remove vibromill process

      4. Used rolled hard material RC 22 on Part Number 346543

      5. Discuss changing from present vibromill specification to an alternate deburring method on Part Number 456876. Cost reduction would be based on acceptance of new method by Company Z

   B.   Indirect savings would be

      1. Water treatment system within the company

      2. Automate rust preventative and packaging (require capital investment)

      3. Reduce the required paperwork needed to be a Company Z supplier

      4. Reduce inventories of raw materials

      5. Better control of purchased materials through several new computer programs

IV Technology Roadmap

   A.   Water soluble lubricants to improve on environment and part washing capabilities

   B.   Design more machines to do more than one operation

   C.   Improve on cell manufacturing

We are hopeful that the above information meets Company Z's expectations, and we are looking forward to a continued successful business relationship. Thank you

Sincerely,

John Baker
ABC Engineering Company

FIGURE 10: THE WRAP-UP AND FUTURE-NEEDS SLIDE MUST DELIVER A ROBUST CONCLUSION SO THAT THE PROJECT MAY SHOW SUCCESSES BUT ALSO A PATH TO CONTINUE IMPROVING WITH THE SAME PROGRAM.

CHAPTER 20
ASSESSMENT

1. **Presentations are a direct reflection on whom?** The presenter, no matter what, so practice, practice, practice.

2. **What ensures that a presentation will be received favorably?** Being prepared with information that covers your subject, knowing your material, keeping the wording simple, reiterating your point near the end of the presentation, and ending on a salient point to sell your message.

CHAPTER CHALLENGE

Find and write about an infomercial that could be made into a PowerPoint presentation.

THE LAW AND MANAGEMENT

66 *Good intentions can often lead to unintended consequences. It is hard to imagine a law intended for the workforce known to Henry Ford can serve the needs of a workplace shaped by the innovations of Bill Gates.* — Tim Walberg 99

CHAPTER PREVIEW

1

The smallest things may turn into a legal headache.

2

Discrimination now covers an assortment of situations.

3

Labor has a lot of laws.

When I was 11 years old, I found out that what appears to be elementary, in legal terms, may not really be so elementary. When my mother registered me for school, she listed my name as a nickname, the same name as my father. By this time I was aware that my father had abandoned us as a family. I wanted no part of him or his name, so I printed my legal name on homework papers.

Soon, the teacher told me that I could not write my legal name on my homework. I argued that it was my legal name. The teacher still would not let me do it, so things came to a head, and I was told to bring in my birth certificate, or I would fail my classes.

At 11 years old, something so innocuous surprised me so much that I could not believe the trouble that I was causing, but I stood my ground. My mother gave me my birth certificate, so I took it to school, and my teacher was shocked. After a trip to the office with the teacher, the principal, who was a bit taken aback, agreed to change the school records. The teacher was not pleased with me for being right, but it all worked out.

> **The differences between practical assumptions and legal realities may be slight but may be quite important.**

The differences between practical assumptions and legal realities may be slight but may be quite important. A manager has a responsibility, regardless of whether he enjoys legal matters, to know what laws affect his company, as they relate to his position, or to know whom to contact when a problem arises. This is critical in management today.

Old laws change, and new laws are implemented all the time to protect employees. In most cases, management is guilty until proven innocent. As callous as this statement may seem, remembering it may keep a manager out of trouble.

An example of this might involve a discrimination lawsuit. No matter how much a manager thinks that she does not discriminate, it is easier for an employee to claim discrimination than it is for an employer to prove that no discrimination has occurred.

As a young manager, I personally found this to be true. I supervised thirty-five employees, ranging from 22 to 55 years of age, of varying races and both sexes. I knew that all people were to be treated fairly, and I thought that I was doing this.

Suddenly, however, after two years in that position, my employer was notified that an employee had filed a lawsuit against the company, and me personally, and that we were allegedly guilty of racial discrimination. I was stunned, but that was just the beginning. After sixty hours of review of all of my documents, warnings, personal notes, and records, at a monetary loss to the company (not to mention the stress), my documented information proved that no discrimination had taken place, and the case was thrown out of court.[35]

I wanted to counter-sue this individual but was made aware of another legal fact, which was that the employee was protected by numerous laws and Acts, such as the Wagner Act of 1935, the Taft-Hartley Act of 1947, the Civil Rights Act of 1964, and the Americans with Disabilities Act of 1990 (see below), which all allowed the employee to say just about anything he wanted and prevented the employer from doing much about it.

These laws were introduced for admirable reasons. Back in the 1930s through the 1960s, plenty of injustices took place with respect to employees.

In my case, however, the employee made false allegations and walked away without any penalty for making them. I could do nothing about it, and the company lost a considerable amount of money having to defend me and itself. This was an eloquent (but not enjoyable) lesson because I recognized that managers have a lot of responsibility to themselves as well as to their employers to know all of the laws that affect the manager and the employees alike.

This is another reason to have an excellent working relationship with the folks in human resources, as they are, or should be, the central point of any organization when it comes to labor laws. I have listed below some of the Acts related to labor:

1. **Wagner Act of 1935:** The Wagner Act of 1935 is known as the beginning of the National Labor Relations Board. This was one of the first government Acts that showed an administration shift toward organized labor. The Act is still in place today and reviews complaints from workers.[119]

2. **Taft-Hartley Act of 1947:** This Act abolished some of the power of the Wagner Act of 1935. It gave management some rights to defend itself versus the power that labor had been given in the Wagner Act. Ultimately, the Taft-Hartley Act made it more difficult for unions to form and was implemented to offset the Wagner Act.[119]

3. **Civil Rights Act of 1964:** This Act is known as the beginning of Equal Employment Opportunity laws and was one of the most compelling and influential laws of its time, being put in place to prevent discrimination. This law has undergone numerous revisions over time, covering age, disadvantage, and more.[43]

4. **Americans With Disabilities Act of 1990:** The Americans With Disabilities Act requires employers to accommodate disabled individuals. This Act has had items added to it over the years to define disability and is still evolving.[82]

By knowing these Acts, and other laws, managers may begin to understand the gravity of managing employees without causing legal nightmares for themselves and their employers. However, these are not the only labor laws to be aware of. Hundreds of laws, Acts, and court decisions affect day-to-day management.[99]

CHAPTER 21
ASSESSMENT

1. **Why must a manager become like an attorney?** Any little word or gesture may get a manager into legal trouble. A manager must know what to stay away from to prevent future legal situations.

2. **What four Acts are significant to labor?** Wagner, Taft-Hartley, Civil Rights, and Americans With Disabilities.

3. **What is the general theme to all of these Acts?** They govern what management may do in relation to labor. Some limit what management may do, and some give management additional power. They provide an understanding of where labor has been through the years.

CHAPTER CHALLENGE

Choose and write about one law or Act that has benefitted you or been to your detriment.

DISCRIMINATION
Immediate Acknowledgement is Crucial

> *Education is important because, first of all, people need to know that discrimination still exists. It is still real in the workplace, and we should not take that for granted.* — Alexis Herman

CHAPTER PREVIEW

1

Investigate discrimination swiftly.

2

Documentation must be complete.

3

Feedback is a must.

C ompany management is like a four-wheel vehicle. Each wheel represents a different level of management: supervisors, managers, vice presidents, and the president. If one wheel fails, the vehicle goes nowhere. When one manager mishandles a personnel decision, all of management suffers. Age discrimination is the perfect example of a problem that may get out of control.

If not handled correctly, discrimination complaints may cause time loss to management as well as give an employee an incentive to take legal action against the organization.[55] To avoid these predicaments, new managers must learn about all discrimination laws. Key similarities exist in some of these laws, but knowing about them is the first hurdle.[65]

If initial training is not complete or detailed, it is only a matter of time before legal troubles arise. The key is to address problems immediately. Discrimination complaints may be addressed in a couple of ways.

Discrimination complaints may be helpful to a company if handled swiftly and thoroughly. With all of the material covering policy, values, com-

> **Company management is like a four-wheel vehicle. Each wheel represents a different level of management: supervisors, managers, vice presidents, and the president.**

munications, and training, one would think that the message regarding discrimination would be unmistakable to managers, but that is not always the case.

Slowness to react is a killer because when a discrimination complaint is received, a manger may have a short time to investigate and respond. If an investigation is done promptly, this may help to avert the most disturbing and costly problems. Do not take corrective action lightly, as the problem may become more serious.

Why the emphasis on discrimination for managers? If the laws surrounding discrimination are taught correctly, this may save the company millions of dollars. Managers must understand that they are accountable twenty-four hours a day when representing an organization, so what is said may violate even the most unassuming of laws.

On the other hand, action, or inaction, taken by a manager may be as damaging, so the management of a company must be explicit about how to avoid poor company decisions by all of its managers and to respond immediately if a discrimination issue arises.

Two forms of complaints may constitute a problem for a manager. One is an internal complaint submitted via a company complaint form, normally through HR. The second is an official complaint to the U.S. Department of Health and Human Services (HSS).[55]

The first allows the top-acting manager in any given department to attempt to resolve the problem before it becomes an official complaint.[99] The manager has a short time (I normally give myself ten days or less) to begin an investigation. Per the Code of Federal Regulations, Title 45, Section 91.42, the complainant has 180 days to file an official complaint with HHS.[55]

Investigation processes should follow the Code of Federal Regulations, Title 45, Section 91 because if a resolution is not reached, all parties will be at the mercy of what HHS may find during an official discrimination investigation.[55]

During the management investigation process, two management representatives not associated with the conflict should interview all personnel who are aware of the reason for the complaint. After basic details are gathered and documented, both the complainant and the person at the center of the investigation should be interviewed separately.

All relevant information from all parties involved should be collected. Mid-level management should also interview the accused to determine if overt discrimination has taken place. In other words, did this person know that what they were doing was wrong and did it any way?[65]

Based on the results of an investigation, two resolution options are possible. One, an internal resolution may be formalized in writing, and the complaint will be closed. Two, the complainant may file an official discrimination complaint with HHS.[55] The person accused in the complaint may ask company management for an appeal if the request is submitted in writing within ten days.[99] If the complaint has gone to HSS, it would be up to this agency to make a decision about the accused's request.

In the event of an internal resolution, after sufficient evidence is found that the person accused is actually guilty, the first step of corrective action should be to give him a documented warning.

Second, a training program for the guilty should be authorized as a corrective action. This training program, at a minimum, should cover the area that caused the complaint, such as the guilty making racist or sexist comments. If this training is refused, the guilty should be terminated for just cause.[127]

All of this training must be documented and in accordance with what was agreed upon as part of the settlement with the complainant and as per standard mediation practices.[55] All documents should be filed in the personnel folder of both the complainant and the guilty. For the guilty, this is considered a written warning that could lead to more progressive discipline.[82]

If a second occurrence should take place and an investigation is conclusive that the same person is guilty of continued discrimination, this person should be suspended. After the suspension, additional training should take place with the understanding that this is the person's last chance. Again, document all actions taken related to the suspension, and provide copies to all parties involved.

If executives of the company or HSS determine that management handled the investigation incorrectly, the executives must take immediate corrective action before the case blows up even more.

At this point you may be getting perplexed, which is understandable, but in reality, this is how easily a discrimination case may become confusing. This is why an immediate, thorough investigation must take place.

CHAPTER 22
ASSESSMENT

1. **Even with all of the current labor laws and Acts, why does discrimination continue to be an issue in the workplace?** Slow investigation time frames may produce a bomb, and if the fuse is left to burn, the bomb may explode, leaving management with additional undesirable consequences.

2. **What are the two types of investigations that may be used to verify a discrimination case?** Government and internal.

3. **How may discrimination be reduced or eliminated?** Training, training, training.

CHAPTER CHALLENGE

Find and write about a recent case in which a discrimination issue could have been prevented and why or how.

CASE STUDY 2

DISCRIMINATION

CASE GOALS

1	**2**	**3**
Awareness that discrimination may become a federal case.	Knowing that a simple problem may turn ugly.	Understanding that all discrimination cases are a priority.

I have been involved with one federal case, which my employer won because we had the documentation to prove our case. But what I learned was to jump on the case swiftly to avoid severe repercussions.

Two other discrimination cases within the company serve as excellent examples of the effectiveness of quick action. The first case involved a new employee, an African-American night guard, who discovered a miniature noose hanging near one of his check-in points. He immediately reported this to his supervisor, who then reported it to me.

My company's mid-management group had a choice to either decide that no harm was meant and let it go or address it. We decided to hit it head-on. We put all employees who worked in the area on notice and interviewed all of them with other members of management present. People from that area sensed that we were not playing around.

The person who made the noose came forward and claimed that it was a joke, nothing more. A report was put into his file, and he had to apologize to the guard for his actions.

The guard was pleased with the swift action taken by management. We found out later that he had been contemplating further action if nothing was done initially.

In the second case, after working together for years, a male employee began calling a female employee sexual pet names. Again, when the supervisor heard what was going on, he immediately investigated all parties who could have been involved. Within two days, he and I determined what had happened, and other managers re-interviewed the male employee, who admitted that he might have used some inappropriate language.

He was disciplined at the request of the person affected by his actions. There was no documentation of any previous disciplinary problems in his personnel file, so a notice was put into his file, and a notice was posted throughout the plant that this type of behavior would not be tolerated. The point was made definitively and likely prevented future incidents.

> **Speed, multiple interviews, and consequences, some of which may not be pleasant, may help to avoid legal troubles...**

Speed, multiple interviews, and consequences, some of which may not be pleasant, may help to avoid legal troubles that might build up due to inaction.

In both of these cases, the employees who were discriminated against were pleased by how management addressed their grievances.

Being unresponsive to the complaint would have resulted in an official inquiry from a government agency, such as the EEOC (Equal Employment Opportunity Commission). We would have had to interview more personnel in our plant, and then the government would have conducted its own interviews. The company would have been required to officially respond to the government and could have been fined and or required to compensate employees for damages. During this whole process, the company would have had to hire a costly defense attorney, so swift action far outweighed slow responses and long court battles.[35]

CASE STUDY 2
ASSESSMENT

1. **Why did these cases not involve the government?** Both cases were dealt with immediately. This was the best outcome for the victims, and both victims were satisfied in the end.

2. **Where could training have prevented the race and sexual harassment cases?** Employees would have known that physical threats or verbal comments could be taken in more than one way and that subjects such as sexual harassment and one's race are taken seriously.

CHAPTER CHALLENGE

Find and write about a training program that is geared toward preventing workplace discrimination.

23

AUDITS
A Manager's Eyes

CHAPTER PREVIEW

1	2	3
Managers may not see everything.	Audits are an extension of management.	Audits keep people honest.

Managers new and old aspire to avoid problems before they occur. Problems with personnel, discrimination, quality, production, and much more may all be detected with audits, which allow a manager to see what happens when she isn't present. Numerous guidelines must be followed when performing an audit, but two easy ones are The Department of Labor's self-audits[112] and the American National Standard Quality Management System Requirements, which offers more organizational guidance.

As discussed in previous chapters, training is the key to the utilization of audits. Personnel from all ranks of an organization may be sent to appropriate training sites, such as the U.S. Office of Personnel Management.[128] While a substantial amount of advertising and published information concerning manufacturing and auditing is available, it is not limited to manufacturing. The below example may be used in service, food, and retail businesses as well.

After being trained in how to conduct audits, a manager must then learn when and how often to audit. A manager will normally have input in creating a checklist for recurring audits. By taking a sample audit of procedure, policy, part dimensions, and so on, a manager may check the reliability (or unreliability) of a whole sample.

> **Auditing is a valuable tool that managers should embrace and use often.**

With a fifteen-minute audit, a manager may find a comfort zone instead of detailing a process that could take hours or even days to complete. This kind of audit saves a lot of time and expense.

A secondary use for an audit is that the results may be documented on an official audit form. Normally, results are published both to management personnel and employees, showing transparency of information. The department manager logs all completed audits and also indicates the purpose for the audit. This reinforces the manager's decisions about which areas of the department need or do not need attention. Human resources must be aware of all audits, as they help HR to understand personnel issues that may arise.[82]

To reiterate audit importance, in 2002, President George Bush signed the Sarbanes-Oxley Act into law. This Act focused on public companies' finances and securities. It requires a chief financial officer to sign off on reports before they are sent to the government.

A primary component of this Act is that an audit committee must be established to oversee actions taken by the company to verify compliance with the Sarbanes-Oxley Act. The audit committee may not include a director, an officer, a partner, or an employee of the company, and management is notified when the audit committee is present in the office.[104]

Auditing is a valuable tool that managers should embrace and use often. It is the best method for checking to make sure that everything is working as it should be without the manager being present all day every day. It also allows corrective measures to be taken to avoid legal ramifications related to safety, finances, and personnel.

CHAPTER 23
ASSESSMENT

1. **How may a manager see everything?** A manager may not see everything, but what a manager may do is learn to use the tool that is an audit. Snapshots in time let a manager know if a problem has surfaced without being on the job 100 percent of the time.

2. **What may an audit help confirm?** Lawfulness in maintaining control and support and making sure that legal requirements are being followed. This includes manufacturing and service settings.

CHAPTER CHALLENGE

Where do you think an audit would help in your employment setting?

24

CONFLICT HAPPENS

> *A good manager doesn't try to eliminate conflict; he tries to keep it from wasting the energies of his people. If you're the boss and your people fight you openly when they think that you are wrong--that's healthy.* — Robert Townsend

CHAPTER PREVIEW

1	2	3
Be ready for anything.	If something happens, you must immediately have a second option.	You must address conflicts.

The old saying that *shit happens* is true, but a skilled manager will adjust to situations as they take place. Some conflicts you can plan on, but most will be a surprise.

At 15 years old, my friend Peter and I were walking down the street at roughly 11:00 at night. Ten not-so-nice people, whose interests did not concern our health and wellbeing, confronted us. Several minutes, a broken nose, and two black eyes later, I learned some lessons that came in handy later in life and on the job. Plan ahead, have a backup plan, and understand what you are getting into before you jump in. As a 15-year-old, sometimes lessons are learned a bit too late and at a painful price.

These painful lessons have stuck with me and have paid dividends. One year after being promoted to manufacturing manager, I terminated an employee who had a history of being unstable. Remembering his past conflicts, I called the local police department and asked ahead of time for backup. I was informed that the officers could not come into the building but that they would be at the company's fence line. If they were flagged in, they could enter the building.

Other company personnel and I fashioned a signal system that went through four different people. If the termination didn't proceed well, I could activate the signal system.

> **Even what may appear to be a minor harassment case may become more grave...**

Two managers and two labor representatives met with the employee. The first five to ten minutes went smoothly, but then things soured. Concluding that management had made its decision and that his termination was deemed final, the now ex-employee became irate.

I scratched the side of my nose with a slight downward motion of my head, and within two minutes, two police officers jogged into the building. The terminated employee was escorted to his locker, where he removed all of his personal possessions, and was forcibly removed from the building.

The two officers also noticed that he had two rifles mounted in the back window of his truck. No one knew what he would have done.

This sounds like a story that could be in the headlines today. If I had not had my early brush with physical conflict, it would be difficult to say if I would have taken this case as seriously as I did.

Conflict takes on different forms. Physical conflict is a concern, and physical aggression has no place in a work arena. Physical conflict normally results in termination because if a person causes a physical altercation once, he will likely do it again. This becomes a zero-tolerance proposition.

Harassment is another form of conflict that may become physical but tends to be, or at least begins as, an emotional matter. This type of conflict is more difficult to defend and get to the bottom of. It tends to be a he said/she said affair, and the company must get to the facts as quickly as possible, as these problems may escalate as time goes on.

Companies tend to lose a lot of time trying to find out all relevant information. If management does not speak with the person causing the problem, fines, penalties, and lawsuits may become a considerable expense.

Another time, one of my employees wanted to wear a T-shirt with the phrase *blow people away* printed on it, and this same guy made comments about how he could get rid of people by blowing them away.

After more than forty hours of investigation by three members of management, with discussions with company attorneys, it was determined that this one T-shirt was inappropriate but others were not, and that some comments that he had allegedly made about coworkers were, in fact, hearsay.

The members of management had a meeting with this individual and made the company's policy quite clear. Harassing comments and T-shirts with gory sayings on them were not acceptable. This guy did receive a warning for his actions, and the company posted its concerns on all bulletin boards, reminding employees that this type of harassing behavior was not acceptable.

Even what may appear to be a minor harassment case may become more significant, so management must take all actions necessary to get to the bottom of things immediately.

Sometimes conflicts happen because management makes decisions that labor does not agree with, which may cause as many (if not more) issues than employees' physical altercations. An example of this is found in a recent case involving Boeing. Please see the next Case Study.

CHAPTER 24
ASSESSMENT

1. **No matter what, a manager cannot stop all conflict, but what could a manager do in case of a conflict?** Be aware of what is around you. Do not bury your head in the sand and hope that conflict will go away. Address the conflict before it gets out of hand. Call for assistance if a problem becomes overwhelming. Remember that even though you did not cause the problem, you need to control it.

2. **Some employees will push the limits to see how far they can go. Should you let them?** If you let a situation go, it will escalate and may become a hell zone. It may be uncomfortable at first, but the sooner you address the conflict, the better it will be for you and your employees.

CHAPTER CHALLENGE

Find and write about both a conflict that was addressed and one that grew out of control.

INTENTIONS

CASE GOALS

1	**2**	**3**
Managers may not always say what they meant to say.	Perfect intentions may be viewed by others as poor choices.	When the government gets involved, rules become blurry.

Boeing's latest project, the completion of its first production run of the Dreamliner, was anything but a dream. It is fitting that Boeing's largest, most advertised project is running into union troubles. Before examining Boeing's recent project, the history between Boeing and the International Association of Machinists (IAM) must be reviewed.

In 2001, Boeing moved its headquarters from Seattle (where its assembly plant is still located) to Chicago and also continued significant operations in twenty-six states in the U.S. alone, making its decentralization from Seattle apparent.[135] Boeing has weathered five union strikes over the last thirty-seven years, including a fifty-two day IAM-led strike over Boeing getting outside-supplied parts delivered right to the assembly line in 2008 (this resulted in

IAM members receiving an impressive monetary settlement).[113,131] This sets up the latest chapter in the Boeing-versus-IAM saga.

Boeing never imagined that 2011 would turn out to be a wild year. Little trouble was anticipated when a strategic plan was conceived with the board of directors to build a second aircraft assembly plant in South Carolina. This was fabulous news for South Carolina, which happens to be a right-to-work state (employees do not have to join a union), but it did not last long. A maze of legal paperwork began before anyone knew who was working where, or at all.

One matter that arose was collective bargaining. The National Labor Relations Board (NLRB) classifies bargaining in three levels: mandatory, permissive, or prohibited. The mandatory stage was at the heart of this case.[88] The IAM felt that moving the assembly plant to South Carolina was part of the labor contract and was based on threats. By moving to a different location, the company would not have to deal with the powerful and disagreeing union members in Seattle.

Boeing and the IAM have had numerous labor battles over the years, so conflict between these two groups was a given. The issue at hand was that the IAM felt that the move out of the Seattle area was a slap in the face to union workers. Boeing did not agree with all of the claims of the IAM.[113]

At the center of this case was whether Boeing had the right to build another assembly plant without negotiating with the union. Boeing claimed that it did negotiate with the IAM. Ronald Meisburg, past NLRB council member, cited in the Bloomberg News:

> *Boeing's statements that it met with the International Association of Machinist and Aerospace Workers, which then lodged a complaint with the NLRB...the irony is that Boeing reportedly did bargain with the union...you bargain and then what happens.*[4]

To top things off, what became a main argument in the disagreement was that Boeing executives were heard making comments that they were moving in order to get away from the Seattle union because of past labor strikes.[4,113] This showed the intent to undermine the union by moving away from the union's control to a non-union environment. In the end, Boeing was allowed to keep the South Carolina plant but had to agree to add work to its Seattle facilities.[78]

To compound the problem, this case had an added twist, government involvement. The NRLB, which is itself unionized, oversees the rights of union workers through the National Labor Relations Act of 1935.[88] The last several years have seen more Democratic appointees to the board, which means that the

> **The lesson here is that once words come out of someone's mouth, they may not be taken back.**

board is pro labor. The NRLB's judgments are not supposed to be political, but past decisions show that it has been difficult to separate the NLRB from politics.[113]

A case between the Embarq Corporation and the American Federation of Labor and Congress of Industrial Organizations over Embarq's relocation from Las Vegas to Florida held sway on the Boeing case decision. The NLRB concluded that *the law does not compel the production of information on relocation decisions to a union.*[4] If Boeing had lost the lawsuit, it may have been forced to build another plant in Seattle to house another production line.

From the viewpoint of some, executives at Boeing blew it. The lesson here is that once words come out of someone's mouth, they may not be taken back. A manager may want to blurt out personal comments or opinions during especially frustrating moments, however, even if the comments have some element of truth to them, this truth may be blown to smithereens, and this is what happened at Boeing.

Before the litigation was settled, it was said that the case would change labor relations forever. Boeing executives had concerns in this case because if Boeing lost, additional guidelines would surely be implemented that companies with unionized employees would be required to follow.

CASE STUDY 3
ASSESSMENT

1. **Case Study #3 illustrates a different type of conflict. What in Case Study #3 is similar to Case Study #2, and what is different?** The similarity is that verbal comments offended employees of the company. The difference is that this case involved an executive level of management, which proves that no level of management is immune from conflict.

2. **Again, knowing now that most conflict may be avoided or limited, do you think that the controversy in Case Study #3 could have been prevented?** Yes. This case showed that no matter where a manager falls on the management chart, if he does not think before he opens his mouth, things may go from bad to worse. If executives at Boeing had kept their mouths shut, this case would have been a much less significant conflict.

CHAPTER CHALLENGE

Find and write about another case where an executive made comments that created conflict.

PROBLEM-SOLVING METHODS

CHAPTER PREVIEW

1	**2**	**3**
Know the difference between a simple and a complex decision.	Multiple aids are available to help solve problems.	Managers must make lists.

Some decisions are easy to make, while others may appear easy but are often difficult. When I was 21 years old, I made the cut on a semi-pro football team as a linebacker. I worked hard to make this team. Playing professional football was a goal of mine as I grew up.

Prior to the first game, I popped a hamstring, and when I say popped, that is exactly what I mean. The decision that I had to make was not intricate. Either my short semi-pro football career was over and I should move on, or I could heal up and try again. Yes, I decided that my football career was over.

Some management decisions are uncomplicated. However, there may be a fine line between uncomplicated decisions and those that require some deliberation. We have discussed some critical areas of management that should not be taken lightly, such as harassment, violence, motivation, and so on, that involve deep thought and necessary action by the manager.

Other decisions, who is going to work what hours, which operator is better for a certain job assignment, are essential but may be figured out somewhat automatically with limited tragic results. Both types of decisions are necessary, but the challenge in decision-making is more distinctly felt when the decision is more difficult to make.

Every year, more books, articles, and studies concerning decision-making are published,

> **Some management decisions are uncomplicated. However, there may be a fine line between uncomplicated decisions and those that require some deliberation.**

so obviously confusion still exists as far as which decision-making methods are the best. Below is a brief breakdown of methods developed for manufacturing; however, they may be valuable for any business:

1. **8D:** Define the problem, measurement method, containment, identify root cause, identify corrective action, implement corrective action, verify effectiveness of action, and prevent recurrence.

2. **Seven Diamond Process:** Correct process, correct tool, correct part, part quality, process change needed, design change required, and statistical engineering needed.

3. **5 Whys:** Identify at least five reasons why a problem was not prevented, then five reasons why the process was not protected, and five reasons why the process was not predicted to fail.[1]

4. **Fishbone (Ishikawa) Diagram (Figure 11):** This is also known as a Cause-and-Effect Diagram, which is structured like fish bones with key points listed at the ends of the bones. A typical set of categories includes methods, equipment, people, materials, measurement, and environment.[6]

5. **SWOT:** Strengths/Weaknesses/Opportunities/Threats, which will be broken down in later chapters.

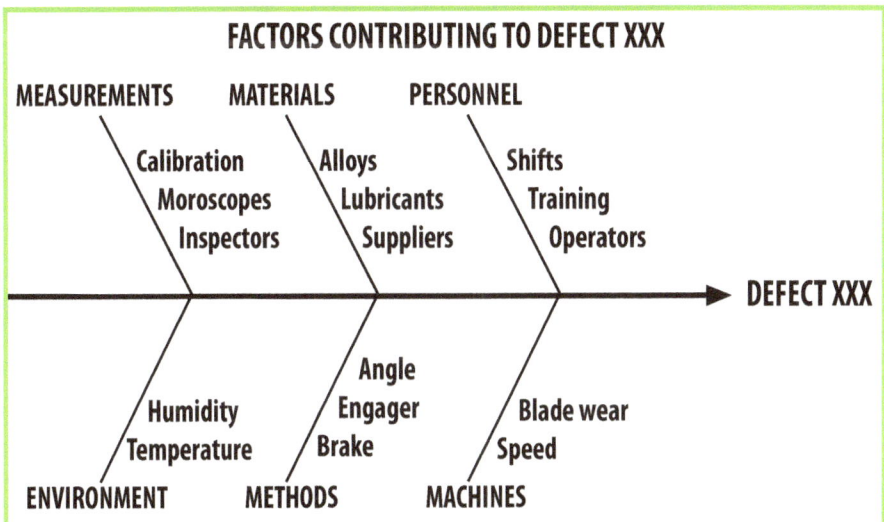

FACTORS CONTRIBUTING TO DEFECT XXX

MEASUREMENTS — Calibration, Moroscopes, Inspectors
MATERIALS — Alloys, Lubricants, Suppliers
PERSONNEL — Shifts, Training, Operators

DEFECT XXX

ENVIRONMENT — Humidity, Temperature
METHODS — Angle, Engager, Brake
MACHINES — Blade wear, Speed

FIGURE 11: BASIC FISHBONE DIAGRAM, USED TO TRY TO GET TO THE REAL CAUSE OF A PROBLEM.

The list of problem-solving methods goes on and on. Most of these models use the same basic concepts:

1. List the problem with a minimum of five possibilities, not the symptoms but the actual problem (in some cases it may be difficult to discern between the two).

2. A group of company thinkers identifies as many possible corrective options as may be thought of.

3. Evaluate which options have the most positive and/or negative effects on the problem.

4. Make a decision in which direction to go. Write a list from most to least possible choices.

5. If plan A does not work, check it off as a not-viable trial, and go on to the second best choice from step four above[1]

This would appear to be straightforward, but even the least detrimental problems may trip up the best thinkers. The first reason that wrong decisions are made is often because the symptom of the problem has been identified as the problem itself. Investigations do not go deep enough for those doing the investigating to see the real problem.

Again, the above examples may seem to be for manufacturing, but they are not. Communities and schools occasionally run hazard or tornado exercises, and when the exercise is over, authorities are supposed to review how the exercise worked. Depending on the complexity of the exercise, the problem-solving component may vary, but the steps found above may still be used, such as listing five reasons why the plan did not work as well as anticipated or five ways to make it work better next time.

After the exercise, upper-level management draws up a fishbone to list all possible items to change based on information possessed before the exercise. To conclude, top management may construct a SWOT table so that all information relevant to determining how to make the whole program better may be seen.[5]

CHAPTER 25
ASSESSMENT

1. **To assist in solving problems, a manager must have some foundational tools that she may use to resolve concerns without wasting time, such as?** 8D, Seven Diamond Process, 5 Whys, Fishbone Diagram, and SWOT

2. **What is the theory behind using problem-solving tools?** To encourage people to list real problems, identify what the problem is, evaluate, make a decision, and have a follow-up plan.

3. **Which plan sounds the easiest but, in fact, is the most burdensome?** The 5 Whys sounds easy, but try it. Identify five reasons why the problem was not prevented, five reasons why the process was not protected, and five reasons why the process was not predicted to fail.

CHAPTER CHALLENGE

Other than SWOT, which will be covered later, use one of the methods listed above to solve an everyday problem.

26

INVESTIGATE SOLUTIONS

Good management is the art of making problems so interesting and their solutions so constructive that everyone wants to get to work and deal with them. — Paul Hawken

CHAPTER PREVIEW

1

The first answer to a problem is not always the best answer. Be open to other possibilities.

2

Do not initially make one answer the final answer.

3

Most real solutions are not easily seen.

With even limited experience, most managers will be able to recall times when they thought that a problem had been resolved but then found out later that it still existed. The problem-solving methods described above guarantee that errors in judgment will at least be minimized.

One operator machining steel parts created a large number of pieces that did not conform to customer requirements and would not work correctly when used. When something crops up that causes damage or a large monetary loss, management personnel are sent in to determine what is causing the problem. This investigative group could consist of one to three management members.

The managers in this case asked the operator why she was producing bad parts. The operator stated that she did not know why the parts were bad but that suddenly the parts were out of tolerance.

The investigators then filed a report blaming poor training. Believe me, training is a factor in scrap and loss profits, and that may be why the investigation stopped there. Another manager doubted this report because of the narrow scope of the report and sent out another investigator, suspecting that there was more to the story.

Remember, there should be more than one possible answer to every question. Look for at least five possible reasons for an error. The second investigator watched the operator and followed each step of the operation. This investigator questioned the operator about each step: the checking device being used, the training that she had received, her knowledge of the machine that she was using, and the times of days when the parts were run.

It was then that the problem became apparent. The checking device seemed to be working correctly but sometimes bounced around. The investigator had someone look at the gauge and found that the hardened tips on the gauge were worn and loose. This caused the readings to change after every use.

Problems are not always this easy to see. When forming steel, machines use pressure to maintain sizes, similar to how restaurants maintain consistent settings in the kitchen so that the same dish doesn't come out different each time.

However, the question chain followed in the example above (instruction, training, temperatures, setting tolerances) doesn't always provide the answer. In this case, everything had been set correctly, and instructions were clear and were followed. Preventive maintenance with secondary devices must be performed on machines, controls, and all equipment in general.

Sometime businesses put controls in place to try and detect problems before they become huge crises. This does not correct the problem, but it prevents the problem from growing. Auditing cash registers in stores does not detect who did what, but it identifies a potential loss before it gets too far out of control.

The point here is that problem-solving takes time up front, but it may save investigative time and money exponentially later. A manager needs to get team members to think about what is taking place. In the above case, the first investigator was too narrow-minded, as the problem originated not with the operator but with maintenance. The problem-solving team must be cross-functional and unafraid to express their ideas. Remember, at least five ideas for each problem must be submitted in order to challenge all members of the team.

The Fishbone Diagram and SWOT methods provide even more ways to find a solution to a problem. The Fishbone method is one of the basic methods of solving problems. It may be done individually, but it is mainly used as a team-building practice. A seasoned manager uses this concept when thinking about problems in his head, whereas new managers are better off documenting their ideas on paper, so that they may better see and organize their thoughts.

The idea is to draw a fish with bones coming off of a central backbone (Figure 11 above). Each bone sticking out becomes an idea. Each idea forces people to think deeper and harder about every possibility that could have gone wrong. This may become a long list. Then the team discusses and analyzes every idea until the group has planned its A, B, and C approaches to tackling the problem.[6]

Idea A is tried out or investigated, and the group then re-visits the original problem to see that all corrections made have worked. If not, idea B is then tried.

SWOT (Strengths, Weaknesses, Opportunities, and Threats) is primarily used for strategic purposes. But it is also a significant factor indecision-making. Lower levels of management use this tool in a limited fashion, but it is an especially meaningful tool when dealing with personnel.

We will discuss the basics first so that the concept is fully understood. Other uses for SWOT will be shown later in the book.

SWOT

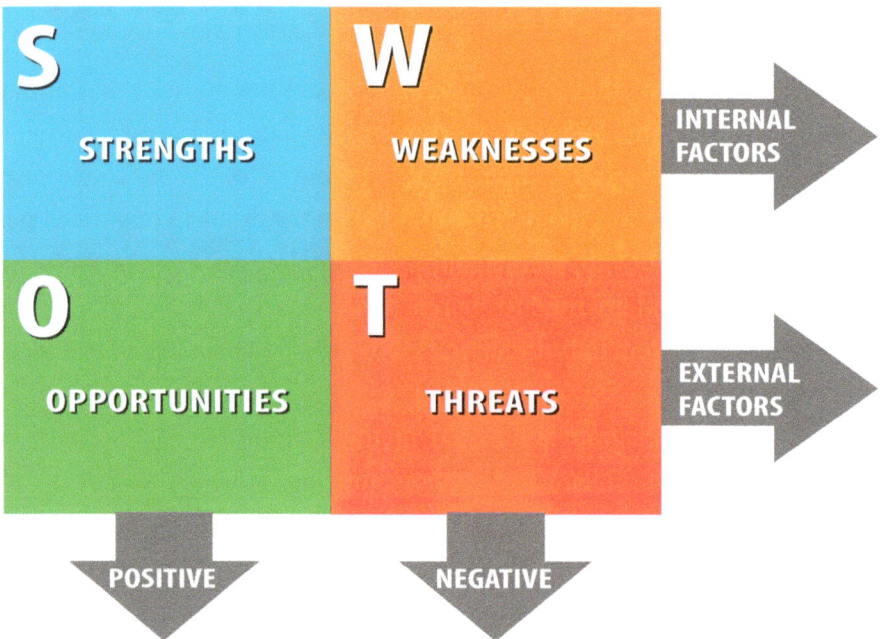

1. **Strengths:** What is the strongest stance that a manager may take when correcting an issue? If an individual is a loose cannon, the manager's physical presence will mean nothing, but a well-mannered conversationalist may be able to smooth over emotional differences. The manager must know his own strengths.

2. **Weaknesses:** As stated above, physical presence may not be effective because if a manager is five-foot-five and an employee is six-foot-

three, this may be perceived as a weakness. Understand it and adjust for it.

3. **Opportunities:** This is sometimes taken for granted. An example of opportunity is discipline. How may opportunities be considered when disciplining someone? If an employee violates a work rule and this work rule has not been a problem for some time, this person may be singled out and disciplined for everyone else in the organization to see.

   One rule that is often violated in manufacturing is the wash-up time period. Instead of disciplining everyone, the manager finds the worst offender, disciplines that individual, and then posts a reminder throughout the whole building. This reminds all employees of the rule and places the focus on the person who violated the rule, bringing peer pressure into the mix.

4. **Threats:** Threats is a key element that must be taken into consideration to avoid additional difficulties because in management, threats are always there. A manager will recognize all possible threats ahead of time. Not all threats are physical.

> **...any method used to solve problems must be used religiously in order to see what truly works for each individual under different types of variables.**

A simple computer error may be a threat. This was the case when one company computer system rounded numbers down to a hundredth of a minute. When operators were running jobs that required hundreds of pieces an hour, their pay ended up being short. The worst case was fifty cents in a given day, and this affected 8 percent of all employees.

In reviewing the facts, most management personnel thought that this was a minor problem that had been corrected, but this was not the case. The employees threatened to walk out because they thought that this was an intentional maneuver by management. It took some immediate, fast-talking discussions to avoid a monumental problem. Reviewing possible threats and resolving them as early as possible is vital.[65]

The above SWOT is used somewhat differently than it would be in strategic planning, which we will discuss later, but both methods are relevant when used correctly. However, any method used to solve problems must be used religiously in order to see what truly works for each individual under different types of variables. After years, it becomes obvious what works, but a manager may also learn as much by discovering what does not work and then adjusting his practices. As in life, remember, more foresight causes less hindsight and chaotic adjustments, so always try to plan ahead.

CHAPTER 26 ASSESSMENT

1. **Basic problem-solving methods listed in the previous chapter (8D, Seven Diamond Process, 5 Whys) are structured methods to help in thinking about and delving into a problem, but what two methods require deeper and more involved research?** Fishbone and SWOT

2. **What method requires discussing problems and solutions?** The Fishbone Diagram gets people together and, in an orderly manner, they call out problems and possible solutions, and then these points are listed on the fish, and from there the fish is completed. Then the group goes back and thins out the possibilities until a decision is made.

3. **What makes a SWOT different than other problem-solving methods?** A SWOT (Strengths, Weaknesses, Opportunities, and Threats) requires a manager to think about the first level of management. The Strengths and Weaknesses may sound fairly effortless, but to really consider Opportunities and Threats, a manager must understand the entire business. In utilizing the SWOT method of problem-solving, a manager is improving her odds of advancement.

CHAPTER CHALLENGE

Write about where and how you would use a SWOT.

27

PERFORMANCE IS KEY

In a growth mindset, challenges are exciting rather than threatening. So rather than thinking, oh, I'm going to reveal my weaknesses, you say, wow, here's a chance to grow. — *Carol Dweckn*

CHAPTER PREVIEW

1

A performance review does not necessarily involve offering more money.

2

Performance reviews are meant to open communications.

3

Performance reviews help establish levels of competence.

Any number of performance review sheets may be used for an array of professions or by individual organizations for specific purposes. And all people who perform personnel reviews must understand the real purpose for the review. The primary reason for a performance review is to communicate to an employee how they are doing and what more needs to be done, not to evaluate income.

Yes, most people may think that the word review means a raise, but it does not necessarily. Money may play a role, but it does not have to be taken into account in all performance reviews. A manager must explain to an employee where their performance is in the context of the overall organization. This keeps the employee alert as to whether things are going smoothly.

Reviews (and raises) may be given more often than annually, but employees frequently have the expectation that reviews are being performed to evaluate promotion and raise statuses, so employees must be told at the out-set that wages are paid based on overall performance, but not necessarily considered during each review. Making this policy transparent may prevent hurt feelings and inflated expectations.

New employees are initially informed of what is expected of them, however, new employees have a number of things to learn, so a preliminary review should be given after they have been doing their job for ninety days. After the first review, employees may be judged by how they complete their required tasks and how they achieve their goals of working individually, working as a team member, attendance, attitude, and more.

Individuals' goals may affect other areas of the business, so they are linked to the big picture. Some critical factors should be kept in mind when giving a performance review:

1. There must be a backbone to the performance review process.

2. Goals must be stated so that the individual has a chance to achieve them.

3. The measuring mechanism must be evident to all involved.

Remember, money is not a part of all reviews. Increased wages or benefits may result from a satisfactory review, but it is the outcome of the performance review that the manager is looking for. If the outcome is favorable, then money may be offered. In my years of experience, I have seen that money does make an impression prior to, during, and shortly after a review, but not for the entire period between reviews. This does not mean that money should not be offered; rather it is the timing in how it is offered.

Money is not the only way to pay employees. Other incentives and benefits, such as time off or contribution to a 401(k), are valuable to employees as well.[82]

Performance is a difficult thing to keep at a high level. Some managers assume that when people get hired or promoted into management, they are automatically driven to improve systems, but that is not always the case. Discernible programs must be in place so that all employees understand that if they do not achieve certain goals, discipline of some kind will result. When discipline is necessary, managers must be consistent, and HR should be involved as a neutral party.

The managers at ABC Engineering Company decided that an employee would complete a self-survey first if discipline was necessary. This allowed the employee to state his/her case, and the manager could then review to see if something had been overlooked. The manager would also have time to consider what the employee documented and either verify or disprove the statements.

When breaking performance methods down, company management had to decide what it wanted to accomplish, then decide what perks would work best for employees. All businesses need measurements (within the performance review) that help make clear to employees what they are expected to do.

At ABC Engineering Company, operators are paid for each piece produced in manufacturing, or each sale in a service area, and then the company monitors whether at least a minimum quantity is met. The operator has a chance to make a higher wage if the performance is kept at a level higher than the average expected.[82]

> ❝
> ## The feeling of being better than someone else in the organization is compelling.
> ❞

This, of course, does not work with non-production personnel (because the measurements are more difficult), so other performance review methods must be used.

Another approach that could be considered is giving employees incentives. Incentives could include bonuses, commission, or profit sharing.[82] One example of an incentive program is a shipping or sales bonus. The more product shipped, the greater the pay.

A frequent problem with this kind of program is that there are no incentives to ship quality products or to make internal processes more efficient, so other steps must be taken to reinforce other cost concerns.

A third method that may be used to recognize performance is benefits. Typical benefits include extra vacation time, healthcare, increased 401(k) contribution,[82] among other things. Offering benefits allows for a more complete system of measurement and should favor the company on a grander scale. Offering benefits may be used for all business types, as this normally applies to most employees.[82]

A review should cover the aspects of an employee's performance primarily related to economic improvements, both for the individual and the organization. Money is the most obvious economic improvement for an employee, as she may buy things, such as clothes, automobiles, and appliances.[82]

Secondly, strong but subtle, is a psychosocial benefit. When employees compare their performance or pay to other individuals, people who want more will do more. The feeling of being better than someone else in the organization is compelling.[82]

The overall goal for performance programs must be growth. Pay is the beginning, knowing that one is doing better than others puts an individual up one more notch, but the ultimate goal is more responsibility and promotion.

Performance goals build and drive people, but no matter which programs or combinations of programs are used, whoever is responsible for reviews and rewards must stay within governmental laws and good HR practices.[82]

Presented here is an actual and simple performance review form. After the form is filled out, a grand total may be calculated to determine an individual's overall performance (see Figure 12 below):

FIGURE 12: PERFORMANCE REVIEW FORM TO BE FILLED OUT PRIOR TO REVIEW.

SUPERVISOR						
Complete this section prior to conducting the performance review with the employee. To assist the employee with helpful feedback, expand on your ratings with written comments regarding your observations, both positive and negative.						
1 **Job Knowledge & Skills:** Demonstrates the knowledge, skill, and expertise required to perform the job. Stays informed of latest developments in field.	N/A	1	2	3	4	5
2 **Planning & Organizing:** Plans work systematically, establishes priorities, and practices effective follow-up procedures to accomplish current and future activities.	N/A	1	2	3	4	5
3 **Adaptability/Flexibility:** Grasps new ideas and methods and modifies behavior when necessary to maintain effectiveness.	N/A	1	2	3	4	5
4 **Quality of Work:** Is thorough, accurate, and performs work according to expectations and established standards. Shows a positive commitment to the TS program.	N/A	1	2	3	4	5
5 **Productivity:** Organizes work, time, and environment to accomplish assignments within specified time frame and meets production schedule.	N/A	1	2	3	4	5
6 **Problem-Solving/Decision-Making:** Can analyze complex problems, is decisive in making timely and high quality decisions, looks beyond the obvious to find cause.	N/A	1	2	3	4	5

7 **Communication Skills:** Verbal and written communications are clear, concise, and effective.	N/A	1	2	3	4	5
8 **Interpersonal Skills:** Tactful, respectful, and effective when interacting with others. Gives credit where due and provides feedback on suggestions. Good listening skills.	N/A	1	2	3	4	5
9 **Team Work:** Cultivates trust, collaborative with others, and constructively deals with conflict. Enthusiastic and sets a positive example for others.	N/A	1	2	3	4	5
10 **Continuous Improvement:** Provides sound recommendations for cost-saving improvements. Identifies and implements process improvements.	N/A	1	2	3	4	5
11 **Dependability:** Works with a sense of urgency. Utilizes time effectively. May be relied upon to be at work daily to ensure that work assignments are completed.	N/A	1	2	3	4	5
12 **Safety:** Committed to safety practices by complying with all OSHA and Company guidelines. Improves safety in the department. Conducts proper investigations.	N/A	1	2	3	4	5
13 **MRBs:** Has very few. Responds in the required time frame. No repeat occurrences. Expeditiously closes outs all with proper documentation and explanations.	N/A	1	2	3	4	5
14 **Scrap & Rework:** Takes steps to ensure its reduction. Maintains an acceptable level, period after period. Has effective control over it.	N/A	1	2	3	4	5
15 **Training:** Ensures all employees in their department are fully trained to perform all required jobs in their department.	N/A	1	2	3	4	5
16 **Leadership:** Plans and thinks strategically, understands Company dynamics. Identifies and develops employees. Holds quarterly meeting every quarter.	N/A	1	2	3	4	5

Additional Comments:

Prior to an actual review, an employee should fill out a self-assessment form so that both the individual and manager may compare opinions. This allows differences to become more apparent, and the hope would be that the employee and the manager might come to a general agreement by the end of the performance review (Figure 13, on the following page).

ABC Engineering Company Employee Self-Assessment

EMPLOYEE INFORMATION

Employee Name: _____

Title: _____

Supervisor's Name: _____ _____

Date: _____

PLEASE COMPLETE THIS QUESTIONNAIRE, AND BE PREPARED TO DISCUSS IT WITH YOUR SUPERVISOR AT YOUR ANNUAL PERFORMANCE REVIEW.

Accomplishments: Please list your major accomplishments and achievements during the past year. In which areas do you feel that you exceeded your position's standards and/or any expectations? Be specific and give examples.

_____

Growth: Please list the steps that you have taken in the past year to make yourself a more valuable and versatile member of the organization. Include any educational programs that you feel have helped you during this review period.

_____

What do you like most about your job? Please describe what aspect of your job has been most helpful to you.

_____

What do you find most difficult about your job? Please describe any obstacles that may stand in your way of effectively doing your job.
Performance Goals: Please list the goals that you would like to accomplish during the next year.

_____

Developmental needs: Please identify areas where you feel that you could make improvements, and list the ways in which you will achieve these objectives. Be specific.

_____

Management Support: Please list the ways in which you believe your supervisor could support you in your goals.

_____

Future Career Goals: Please identify your interests beyond your current job/function. Be specific.

_____

Employee Signature: _____
Date: _____

Supervisor Signature: _____
Date: _____

FIGURE 13: SELF-REVIEW SURVEY TO AID EMPLOYEE AND SUPERVISOR IN PARTICIPATING IN A MORE COMPLETE PERFORMANCE REVIEW.

CHAPTER 27
ASSESSMENT

1. **Why do most managers hate giving performance reviews?** The person being reviewed has a different opinion of their performance than the person giving the review. The person giving the review knows that a review may become adversarial, so they tense up or try to avoid giving the review altogether.

2. **How may conflict be avoided when giving reviews?** A pre-review self-survey helps a manager better understand the interviewee. When a company has a structured review program, the person giving the review already knows the position of the person being reviewed.

3. **What one thing helps a manager who must give performance reviews?** Communication between reviews helps the employee know where they are in terms of performance. If a manager expects that giving a review only once a year will be constructive, undesirable consequences may result. Communicate during the year, and document those communications so that the manager may apprise the individual being reviewed of all facets of his performance.

CHAPTER CHALLENGE

What was your worst review and why?

28

STRATEGIC PLANNING

> " *After a business implements a strategy, competitors will react, and the firm's strategy will need to adapt to meet the new challenges. There is no stopping point and no final battle. The competitive cycle continues on perpetually. Produce and compete or perish.* — Thomas Timings Holme "

CHAPTER PREVIEW

1

Strategic planning helps managers see into the future.

2

Many guides help with the strategic planning process.

3

Managers must understand thatthe plan is not done just because it is writtendown.

S trategic planning requires that managers combine all of their knowledge about scheduling, documentation, motivation, and training. This is a key element to being an excellent mid- to upper-level manager. Strategic planning also plays into the future of an organization, as its purpose is to take a company-wide view and move the company to the next level.

Strategic planning is complex, for a variety of reasons, but we will use the simple stone. There must be a purpose for a plan. The purpose might be to correct an ongoing problem, to look toward the future, to determine how to achieve goals, or to improve areas of the business, but no matter the purpose, the plan is the same. The basic format is broken down into three categories: Position, Resource, and Simple Rules (Figure 14).

STRATEGIC PATHS	POSITION	RESOURCE	SIMPLE RULES
1. Logic:	Establish the position or purpose	Obtain resources	Find opportunities
2. Steps:	Identify attraction market	Find vision	Jump into/keep moving
	Locate defendable position	Leverage vision	Seize opportunities
3. Questions:	Where should we be	What should we be?	How to proceed
4. Advantage:	Limited, valuable, combinable	Limited valuable	Key process, distinctive
	Active system	One and only resource	Simple rules
5. Works best:	Show changing, well structured	Moderately changing well structured market	Rapidly changing exclusive markets
6. Duration:	Continuous	Ongoing	Unpredictable
7. Risk:	Too difficult to alter as conditions change	Too slow to build new	Too tentative to executing promising opportunities[9]

FIGURE 14: STRATEGIC PLANNING GUIDE
THREE METHODS OF ATTACK, KATHLEEN M. EISENHARDT AND DONALD M. SULT, JANUARY 2001 HARVARD BUSINESS REVIEW.[104]

Managers must choose which of the three categories they will utilize when setting their strategic plan. If you are looking to attack an outside competitor, then the Resource category may be the best choice because you want to build a leverage vision, and it would be too slow to build new. If a manager wishes to address a need within the organization, it may be better to use the Position category to examine the company's current position or purpose versus where the company should be.[104]

> **Strategic planning requires that managers combine all of their knowledge about scheduling, documentation, motivation, and training.**

These three strategic paths are tools that may be utilized when forging a strategic plan. In the next Case Study, we will see that strategic planning, including topics from previous chapters, falls into place to correct a major problem.

Not all managers have direct input into the strategic plan, but knowing how it is designed helps them to understand how to enforce it, and then perhaps managers may suggest areas that may improve it.

This next Case Study shows why strategic planning is so important and how the skills outlined in this book help managers to build a more rewarding plan. As will be shown, strategic plans may take time. In the following Case Study, the plan spanned more than four years, leading only to a first level of completion. Follow-up to the original plan was an ongoing effort that included updating procedures and policies within the organization, including the company's own strategic philosophy, which was difficult.

Ground rules must be established when an organization decides that it is time to determine a new strategic plan. The plan involves training personnel, which sounds fairly straightforward, and on paper it may even look painless, but putting this well-thought-out strategic plan into action takes work.

Countless numbers of articles, manuals, and books have been written describing how to put strategic plans into action. I have seen both positive and negative aspects of strategic planning that I will point out in the Case Study below.

As the Engineering/QA Manager and the ISO/TS 16949 representative with the International Organization for Standardization at ABC Engineering Company, I was close to the action on both the upper and lower levels of the plan, so I had a unique opportunity to review the plan. As may be seen in the next Case Study, the QA Manager was directly responsible for setting the plan in motion and seeing that all facets of the plan were completed on time. This is why managers must be ready and prepared to take over meaningful programs at any time.

CHAPTER 28
ASSESSMENT

1. **Strategic planning sounds formal and it is, but why should it not be used by first-line managers?** It may be used by all managers. The three-category approach may be used from entire restaurants to a single department. Some in-depth investigation must be done in order to formulate a solid overall plan.

2. **What are you trying to achieve with a strategic plan?** A person, team, or company is trying to ensure the best position for the future.

CHAPTER CHALLENGE

Where would you think a strategic plan would best be used and why?

STRATEGIC PLANNING

CASE GOALS

1	2	3
No matter what, business quality is crucial.	Deming's Fourteen Points maybe used everywhere.	Energy put into strategic planning up front pays dividends later.

Strategic planning may involve suggestions from everyone within an organization. In this Case Study the strategic plan subject is quality, so strategic planning steps are taken to accomplish an overall quality change. This type of plan will also work in every industry, whether manufacturing, food processing, finance, or anything else. Four main topics should be kept in mind when effecting a new quality plan through a strategic planning program:

1. Assessment: organization, task, individual.

2. Objectives and measures.

3. Design and delivery: interference or transfer for on-the-job, off-the-job, and online training.

4. Evaluation.[88]

Many organizations still use W. Edwards Deming's Fourteen Points today, for the purposes of initiating quality changes.[32] Several of his points are key to any strategic plan. Deming's beliefs regarding strategic planning include adopting a new philosophy, instituting training on the job, breaking down barriers between staff areas, implementing a vigorous program of education and self-improvement for everyone, and lastly, putting everyone in the company to work to accomplish the transformation.[32]

Deming's thoughts constitute a decent starting point. Following the recommendation of management Professor Jeffrey A. Mello, who has held administrative positions at numerous universities and received a Ph.D. with awards in organizational behavior, an action plan may then be set in motion.

To assist in this endeavor, as a means of measurement, in the assessment portion of a strategic plan, a list of goals must be created.

This kind of program allowed ABC Engineering to establish goals for the organization and individuals with unequivocal, measurable objectives. However, up to this point, all work had been part of the documented action plan, and the real work with all personnel still needed to commence.

Remember that each manager plays a part in a strategic plan and must be aware of her role in the program as a whole. That is why even a new manager must understand how a strategic plan works.

As Deming stated, the action plan must show that a new philosophy is being adopted. This means that the new philosophy must be communicated to all employees with a solid reason as to why it is being implemented.[32] In ABC Engineering's case, the reason was the final goal of achieving a customer-required ISO 9000/TS 16949 accreditation.

Convincing employees that the philosophy of documenting procedures and policies, when there had been little of this previously, was a whole new approach to business. The initial process was primarily completed with off-the-job classroom training in areas such as statistics, process control measurements, and explaining each ISO/TS procedure.

Also, on-the-job training, like documented work instructions, charts, examples of successful programs, and banners were used to seal the deal.[88] The overall plan was taking shape and gaining support.

During this time period, the program designers intended that managers would keep reiterating the new procedures and policies. Because

> " ...to drive a philosophy change, it is necessary to have a purpose... "

of this, managers and employees heard the program over and over, which got them used to the terms and language used in the program.

After training was completed and specific duties were assigned, the job was half done. Assessments were completed to determine if the learning process had been done in the proper manner and was understood, thereby allowing the strategic planners to decide if the key objectives of the plan were in line to accomplish the ultimate goals.[88] These assessments were needed to ascertain two things:

1. Was the trainer effective, and was the training done in the best way possible?

2. Was the training understood by the trainee, or was the trainee capable of accomplishing the end task?[88]

Again, to drive a philosophy change, it is necessary to have a purpose, and this was where a goal such as getting an ISO/TS accreditation came in handy. The ISO/TS had devised checklists used to determine how well an organization would do in an assessment, so the organization would know whether it could pass an ISO/TS audit. This process is called a pre-assessment audit[21] and specifically deals with training.

There are numerous sections of questions, and if any negative answers are given, the pre-assessment audit fails, and corrective measures must be taken. Assessment checkpoints to show competence awareness and training include:

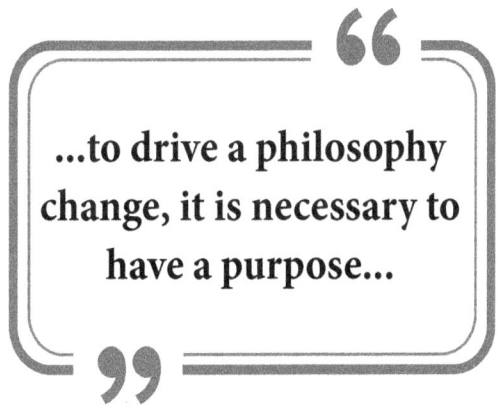

1. Competence levels required for each workstation.

2. Training needs to satisfy requirements.

3. Evaluate effectiveness.

4. Ensure that personnel are aware of the relevance of what they are doing and how they contribute in the final objectives.

5. All training, skill, and experience are documented.[21]

Additional requirements other than those listed above are audited during the pre-assessment process. From this point, an evaluation is made about whether to continue or stop and correct any errors detected.

After assessments are made, the strategic group must evaluate what is or is not working. To do this, the group must review the assessment results and ask the employees if the training was liked and how it could be improved.[88]

When training exercises were completed at ABC Engineering, employees filled out an eighteen-question questionnaire and handed it in anonymously. This enabled management to see what areas of training were understood by those individuals trained and if any subject matter should be changed or added to make the training session better.

This type of feedback is best used to determine if the employees have any interest in the training. If not, it is possible that some employees may not value anything that the company offers, which is information that managers should keep in mind for future personnel evaluations.[88]

In addition to the above-mentioned questionnaires, ABC Engineering also used a second method of evaluation, called a product audit. This involves moving a product produced to an inspection station at which there is an independent auditor. A product audit is especially valuable for new employees, but at ABC Engineering it is performed with seasoned employees as well. This is the truest measurement of what could be expected from the company's training and processing program.[21]

To verify that the strategic plan was on course, additional research was done to confirm that the steps in place had merit, which gave the group confidence that it was on the right track. When analyzing *Quality Magazine*'s top 100 companies for quality leadership, a common denominator was evident. In detail, the top five of those one hundred companies all had similar philosophies:

1. Quality is not someone else's responsibility; it is everyone's.

2. Everyone was eager to make the extra effort to achieve the ISO, TS, or any other certification.

3. Employees were motivated by the established philosophies (direction of the company).

4. The company provided thorough on-the-job training, so employees understood the job and the company philosophy.[107]

Even though the philosophies listed above are on the right track, *Quality Magazine* offered some advice in its article *Don't Punish Employees with Training*. Training was the key point noted above, and it is a critical step in the strategic plan of any business, but when a problem materializes, do not be so fast to blame it on training.

Lots of companies want to use the mistake-blame-train-defend practice.[103] But this causes barriers that should be avoided, as Deming stated, and also causes resistance when trying to train groups in the future. Everyone will remember that training was to blame in the past, so employees may then not have a positive attitude toward training.[32,103]

ABC Engineering's strategic plan dealt with initiating a new company-wide program and brought all employees up-to-date on the whole system. It involved correcting company management practices by looking inward and trying to come to a resolution that everyone could live with. Faulty management practices were an actual, costly problem, and readers should note that the total breakdown in numerous areas is not isolated to this company but is common throughout business.

Managers were needed to enforce each step of the plan. Each one of Deming's points were both enforced by and required motivation from the manager, so this is why managers must understand a company's strategic plan.

Strategic planning is not limited to quality issues. As seen in the next Case Study, a comparison of three companies not in the manufacturing business that had costly breakdowns, each company went in its own direction to negotiate its business obstacles.

The strategic plan detailed in Case Study 4 worked because it involved every level of management. With what you have learned so far, you will be able to determine ahead of time whether each company in the next Case Study is heading in the right direction.

CASE STUDY 4 ASSESSMENT

1. **What is the best way to begin a strategic plan?** Decide how to assess the plan, what the plan objectives are, how to measure them, how the program will be designed and delivered, and the best method of evaluation during and at the end of the program. Be ready to adjust the plan based on the evaluation.

2. **Why are there so many different layers of information within a strategic plan?** One plan does not fit all situations. People involved need to have check points to make sure that the overall steps are being followed and to make sure that the plan is working. This is where the first step of assessments is so critical.

3. **How long should a plan take?** Longer than most people initially think. In this Case Study, it took four years to get to the end of the plan, and even then it was still close to a disaster. But after all was said and done, we at ABC Engineering prevailed.

CASE CHALLENGE

Write about where you think a plan such as the one discussed in Case Study #4 would work and why?

HUMAN RESOURCES

CASE GOALS

1	**2**	**3**
Doing business may be costly when human resources is not involved.	Be aware of all Acts and the laws in your jurisdiction.	Be willing to change, sometimes without delay.

Compliance-based human resource management is the key to a company's legal environment. As the definition implies, structure and direction are given to employees to ensure that employees comply with the rules, regulations, and procedures of the organization.[88] With this type of structure, there is *little employee discretion, and any training, performance management, and compensation would be based on ensuring compliance to the work structure.*[88]

This is especially true in the pharmaceutical business of Walgreens, CVS, and Walmart. The human resources legal culture must be perceivable, as the pharmaceutical business involves heavy regulations and personal health. Liability issues may become severe if all procedures are not maintained within a well-defined structure.

Some of the pitfalls that the above-listed companies must avoid include poor training concerning laws such as the Fair Labor Standards Act, the Health Insurance Portability and Accountability Act, auditing, hospital compliance, and Medicare and Medicaid coverage (and fraud), among others. This area of HR is priceless. If things fall through the cracks in this regard, it may prove quite costly to a company.

In 2008, Walgreens was caught switching prescriptions to more expensive drugs in a scam to defraud Medicaid, which ultimately cost Walgreens $35 million in fines.[90] CVS was charged with a similar crime in the same year. Settling its lawsuit, CVS agreed to pay $36.7 million in fines for improperly switching patients to the more expensive form of Ranitidine for Medicaid reimbursement.[90] In this particular case, a whistle-blower brought the crime to light.[90]

In Walmart's case, a different problem became apparent. Numerous lawsuits pertaining to deaths from incorrectly filled prescriptions were filed against Walmart.[53] This was an HR disaster because of the volume of deadly incidents. There appears to have been a recurring personnel problem.

Employees in a compliance-based environment are trained to follow the rules, so someone had to have known about the incorrectly filled prescriptions, and the HR department was responsible for verifying assessments and evaluations to determine that training did not have shortcomings.[88]

Human resources also has the responsibility of preventing legal problems. The last thing that an HR department wants to do is deal with the Equal Employment Opportunity Commission (EEOC).

Again, Walgreens, CVS, and Walmart have all run into trouble with EEOC compliance. Walgreens was sued for $20 million for discrimination in 2007. By the time the case concluded, however, the $20 million had become $24 million, one of the largest settlements in EEOC history[38] CVS settled an EEOC claim for $55,000 in 2008 that involved both racial and gender job assignments.[39]

However, Walmart has been in the news most lately in relation to discrimination lawsuits, and coming as no surprise, the Walmart pharmacy has been a part of these lawsuits. A Massachusetts jury awarded a female pharmacist $2 million because for eleven years she was paid less than two male pharmacists and was fired when she complained.[110]

Based on the amount of money lost by Walgreens, CVS, and Walmart, justification could be made that each company needs tore-structure its training programs in order to improve the culture and send an unmistakable message to this effect to everyone in the company. It appears that a compliance-based HR management program is not working to its fullest in any of these companies. Programs that were supposed to be structured to make certain that all employees have little discretion and were trained to ensure compliance with all work rules were not working, so all three companies' HR departments had some re-building to do.[88]

One way for human resources to regain respect in the corporate circle would be to implement new or modified strategic plans in order to reduce some of the above struggles. Human resources must play a key role in the construction of a new or modified strategic plan, as shown above, because all three corporations had some expensive shortcomings that needed immediate attention. Corporate management must realize that HR has a duty to consider the implications of problems, both in the present and in the future.[88]

> **Corporate management must realize that HR has a duty to consider the implications of problems, both in the present and in the future.**

In the above cases, human resources departments already had their hands full trying to determine how to repair corporate philosophy. Company management may make dangerous assumptions when trying to recognize the effects that the external environment has on business and, in this case, HR's functions and responsibilities.[88] In short, personnel were not following legal protocols and fundamental training practices, which led to the costly monetary settlements outlined above.

Walgreens made a decision in November 2009 to hire two people, Kathleen Wilson-Thompson, named Senior Vice President and Chief Human Resources Officer, and Charles V. Greener, named Vice President of Corporate Affairs and Communications. This move showed that HR changes that needed to be made were being made.[88, 134]

To make a point to its employees and shareholders, Walgreens published biographies of the two on the Walgreens website, and a press release emphasized the direction in which executives felt the company should go. The highlights of Wilson-Thompson's qualifications included:

1. Member of Kellogg's executive global leadership team.

2. Transformational skills.

3. Leadership ability consistent with dynamic change.

4. Measured approaches.

5. Named in The Top 100 Most Powerful Executives in Corporate America in 2009.[134]

As for Greener, his press release stated that he was known for his vision, had been responsible for government relations, strategic communications, marketing, and investor relations, and had a background in health benefits. The message was clear. A robust communication change was in the wind, beginning with top management down.[134]

A similar change took place at CVS. Michael Ferdinandi was named Senior Vice President of Human Resources. During his term to date, CVS has acquired 3,000 stores, and he has been responsible for navigating the newly-emerging company culture.[98] Ferdinandi also helped design and still oversees The Emerging Leaders Program, which is a series of management training courses that puts the company's stamp on everything.[98]

In addition, Ferdinandi spearheaded an employee-engagement program called Stay and planned to continue to refine it as long he was involved up to and after 2009.[98]

Lastly, Walmart has taken a different approach. No upper-management changes have taken place, at least none that were apparent when reviewing its human resources history. Walmart has increased its communications via ethics programs posted on its website and in handouts.[133] The website does not even list the year that the information was posted or updated, and the only date listed on the site was the Walmart copyright date of 2001.[133] Walmart has a poor corporate human resources image and shows no attempts to address its past problems.

To emphasize this point, a comparison between CVS and Walmart employees' satisfaction was posted on the Internet, with the results following the corporate improvements made at each organization. Of six negative comments, five were against Walmart, and one was against both CVS and Walgreens. Walmart still has a public relations problem in terms of human resources and is making no apparent efforts to change it.[7]

The HR department plays an influential role in making sure that all company personnel are trained and stay within the compliance-based structure in order to maintain strict controls, and this is especially true in the pharmaceutical industry.[88] However, the direction of HR must originate at the corporate level to ensure that proper reinforcement of the rules is carried out.[88] The human resources staff must believe and enforce the Human Resource Management's Code of Ethical and Professional Standards.[88] If this had been followed and sustained, the negative environment mentioned above may have been reduced or eliminated.

Setting HR strategies at the corporate level may serve as a *framework by which an organization may develop a consistent and aligned set of practices, policies, and programs that will allow employees to achieve the organization's objectives*, and also to reinforce *compliance-based* management and avoid legal troubles.[88]

Another one of HR's responsibilities is to ensure that the organization is responsive to change.[88] This is where Walgreens and CVS have made noticeable improvements, whereas it appears that Walmart is stuck in the same old practices, especially concerning the pharmaceutical side of the business.[133] After reviewing Walmart's legal settlements, its HR department should have, at a minimum, demanded a re-design of its drug disbursement program for two reasons:

1. Multiple settlements were made because some of Walmart's customers received incorrect prescriptions, which in some cases resulted in death.

2. A re-design improves motivation and challenges employees.[88] Walmart's business model, which is based on customer savings, as seen in its television advertisements and corporate agreements, may work in the short term, but when personal safety is at stake, business will suffer.[105]

Since 2013, Walgreens, CVS, and Walmart are each traveling in different HR directions trying to garner a bigger market share. If one had to pick the pharmacy that appeared to be moving in the right HR direction, it would have to be Walgreens because it has doubled its commitment to corporate human resources.[134]

However, in 2013 Walgreens found itself in legal trouble again, proving that its long-term corrections were not working.[74] Walmart was still having trouble in the area of compliance. This led to a new internal legal unit being instituted, which will report directly to the executive vice president, general counsel, and corporate secretary Jeff Gearhart[118].

Based on an independent survey taken by www.consumeraffairs.com, through May 5, 2016, Walmart's pharmacy received a rating of 1.3 out of 5, so Walmart still has room to improve.

In the end, CVS has done the best job of staying out of trouble. This proves that HR solutions are not one-time corrections. A manager must watch every day that corrections being made are maintained.

At every step in the above-mentioned errors and misjudgments, managers could possibly have intervened with employees to make sure that they were trained correctly. As stated in previous chapters, manager audits, complaint forms, and personnel reviews might have prevented some of these concerns before they led to hefty fines. This shows the value that a manager may provide to a company if she knows how the program is supposed to operate.

CASE STUDY 5 ASSESSMENT

1. **Case Study #5 brings a number of things to light for management, which are?** Management may be looked at closely and may be made to look foolish if poor or ineffective actions are taken.

2. **Management is out for the all-mighty dollar, right?** Based on Case Study #5, the answer would be yes, but all management is not this way. However, poorly managed companies shine a spotlight on companies everywhere.

3. **Devising a plan or changing a plan itself does not matter. Why?** As has been seen in previous chapters, a plan must get to the real problem, the plan must have action points, assessments must be used to verify that the correct course of action is working, those involved must be shown how the design of the plan will work, and lastly, there should be a component that allows management to evaluate and re-evaluate that the troublesome areas have been addressed. CVS took sizable steps in this regard and had the best results.

CASE CHALLENGE

What additional steps would you have taken to correct the compliance problems at CVS, Walgreens, and/or Walmart?

29

GOALS FOR THE FUTURE

> *Setting goals is the first step in turning the invisible into the visible.* — Tony Robbins

CHAPTER PREVIEW

1

A manager must have extrasensory perception.

2

A goal may be a series of actions taken leading toward one end result.

3

Goals help create motivation.

Everyone should have goals. I learned early on that goals were the best way for me to at least feel that I was not as poor as my family was. For me, setting goals was a cross between dreaming and making the future happen, so I sensed that I had a chance to get out of where I was.

At 12 years old, one of my goals was to own a brand new Chevrolet Corvette. An ambitious goal for a child living in poverty, but nonetheless, it was my goal. I knew that I first needed to graduate from high school to have a chance at achieving this lofty goal, so I did what I needed to do throughout school in order to pass all of my classes. I was not the best student but not the worst either.

After graduating from high school, I worked a variety of different jobs, in some cases more than one on the same day, but always seven days a week.

I realized that if I bought cars in rough condition and fixed and cleaned them up, I could sell them for more than I had paid for them. I worked long days, either at jobs or on cars, and after five years, working two or three jobs every day and buying and selling thirty-five different cars, I bought a brand new Corvette.

My mother then told me that she had known all long that I was going to buy that Corvette. Later, my Corvette turned out to be the down payment on the first house that my wife and I bought. I went from one out-of-reach accomplishment to another. Simply stated, goals are a series of stepping-stones that lead to a final accomplishment. At 12 years old, I never thought that I would accomplish either one of these things, but by using

> **Goals should be challenging but also realistic. They become guides to improving personally...**

the stepping stone idea, I did know that I had to set goals in order to make things happen.

The same is true for managers. During day-to-day activities, managers forget to think about what got them to their present positions and where they want to go from there. Goals should be challenging but also realistic. They become guides to improving personally as well as within the organization.

As a manager, you should encourage personnel who report to you to have goals.[65] Whether goals are annual or semi-annual, all managers must sit down where it is quiet and write down two sets of goals. The first set of goals should be completed in a shorter time frame, normally within one year. The second set of goals should constitute a five-year plan. There may be some overlap in short-term goals becoming long-term goals, but time limits must be a part of any set of goals.[65]

Most young managers tend to think that goal-setting is a waste of time, but after it is done once or twice, most managers discover why it is useful. During busy times, people tend to forget what desires they wanted to fulfill and what efforts they must put forth to reach their final accomplishment. When people pull out their goals or see them on a bulletin board, it reminds them of what they thought was important, and it helps puts them or keep them on course. Goals may be tweaked over time as people learn and become wiser, but written goals keep dreams alive.

These goals may also illustrate accomplishments for employers at review time. Some of the individual's goals should be part of the company's goals. An executive-level manager should set goals for all levels of management to assist in establishing performance standards.[65]

Again, goals should be obtainable in order to keep employees motivated. If goals are not realistic, they will become deterrents, and both the manager and employee will lose motivation.[65] Budgetary, market growth, improved productivity, and other goals maybe used to assist individuals with getting ahead and are vital tools for all levels of management.

The first two Parts of this book covered elements needed to become a manager at any level. Most of the previous Parts dealt with people, because without people, no company can run. Learning how to organize and motivate people 100 percent of the time may be a tiring challenge, but in the end, it is also rewarding.

The next two Parts will cover where new mid-level managers must plan and get more involved in future company focus. This includes long-term planning, finances, and management styles. Achievement-oriented managers must use the previous lessons to mold a company for the future, which means that a manager must know how the company operates as well as external factors that may change the whole structure of a company.

This area of management becomes more intense, but in a different way, because planning and overall knowledge of the business structure runs at a different pace. Some actions must be immediate, while others are slowly planned, as in playing a game of gin rummy. You see your cards and study not what you need but what others are taking and throwing away. This allows the player to see if what was originally expected holds up, or if last minute adjustments are necessary. The person who plays it right wins not only in cards but also in business.

Look at the next few chapters with a broader view to see what mid- to upper-level managers need to know and understand. However, I must warn you about the curse that I have seen over and over again. When managers are promoted, they forget the personal traits that helped them achieve some of their goals. People are the best asset that any manager has at any level, and newly promoted managers sometimes forget that and treat people poorly.

The first lesson in mid-level management is to not forget how to treat people with respect. In seeing that management opportunities are possible, it is essential to understand the past and what worked then, including the contributions of the people that you worked with. Then build on these things, as we will learn about doing in the upcoming chapters.

CHAPTER 29
ASSESSMENT

1. **Goals are like what?** A cross between dreaming and making the future happen.

2. **Why are goals like time travel?** As a manager, you should go back to review the goals that you set previously and see how far you have come. If you do this correctly, you will be amazed at what was accomplished, and you will have a sense that you were seeing into the future when you wrote down your goals.

3. **Is it possible for a manager to prosper without setting goals?** A manager will know that she is becoming successful in her review of her goals and adjustments made to them. Those who do not have written goals will not as easily know where they want to go or if they got there. Odds increase with documented goals.

CHAPTER CHALLENGE

List five of your own goals and why you wish to accomplish them.

PART III

ASSEMBLE YOUR KNOWLEDGE

IMPLEMENT ACTION
WITH OBJECTIVES

A good objective of leadership is to help those who are doing poorly to do well and to help those who are doing well to do even better. — Jim Rohn

CHAPTER PREVIEW

1	**2**	**3**
Not understanding a subject does not mean that you cannot set goals to learn.	The difference between short-term and long-term goals is not just time.	Learn the easy steps to constructing a plan.

When I was in my late teens, I decided to take up snow skiing, so I crafted a short-term objective, which was to learn how to ski without killing myself. The first task was to purchase equipment, which was a shocking lesson in economics, but with some budgeting, I accomplished that goal.

Then I had to find someone to teach me how to ski. This short-term goal led to skiing on local hills. In the first year (after breaking two sets of skis), the short-term objective was met.

This led to a long-term objective, which was to tackle bigger hills, so over the next two years I expanded my skiing experience by going to some respectable ski hills in Wisconsin. However, as most people who ski know, you have not skied until you have skied the Rocky Mountains.

In my early years, skiing the Rockies looked like a goal beyond reach, but two years later, I hooked up with a ski club and traveled to Colorado. On the fourth day of the five-day trip, some of the skiers went to a ski resort called Arapahoe Basin, also known as A-Basin. This is the highest skiing peak in North America, at over thirteen thousand feet. The ski lift ended at the uppermost point of the mountain, and right before I exited the lift, I looked out over all of the Rocky Mountains.

I had an epiphany. An assortment of things rushed through my mind. First, I was about to ski down the highest point of the Colorado Rockies. Second, I was reaching a long-term goal. I had learned how to ski by accomplishing a series of short-term objectives, linking them together to reach this final destination. And lastly, if I could visit such a beautiful place with such a breathless, amazing view, what else could I accomplish?

This was the final stop on the journey to one long-term objective, but the triumph was complete with the knowledge that I could do almost anything. When I returned from my trip, my plans became more aggressive and detailed, which leads us to why objectives are crucial.

A powerful link between strategic planning and organization is objectives. Managers who organize and make strategic plans must communicate with the people who do the work, and that is the purpose of objectives.[104]

The difference between the two kinds of objectives, short-term and long-term, is time. Short-term objectives are normally completed in less than twelve months and are quantitative and specific; with immediate results expected.[104] Short-term objectives assist individuals in implementing strategy in three ways:

1. Short-term objectives help people reach long-term goals, such as 25 percent growth in five years by way of 5 percent short-term annual increases.

2. They generate discussions and agreements that raise concerns and potential conflicts within an organization that need to be confronted annually during a short-term cycle.

3. Short-term objectives assist managers with implementing strategies that allow for measurable outcomes that include specific goals.[104]

These strategies are accomplished by individuals being able to form and measure priorities. Because short-term objectives must be completed in less time than long-term objectives, they tend to be more easily measured in terms of success or failure using specific numbers, like pieces per hour, number of people within an area, or exact money saved. Also, priorities may be established more easily with a detailed picture by ranking which accomplishments make the biggest impact and may be achieved within the shortest period of time.[104]

Long-term objectives normally take on more complex programs, such as striving for zero waste, conserving natural resources, or meeting regulatory compliance. As may be seen, these are arduous tasks, and measuring them may be a challenge. One way to accomplish any long-term objective is to get there by way of a series of short-term objectives, which then cascade the results into a long-term achievement.[104]

Short- or long-term objectives become easier to affirm after strategic plans are in place. Then the purpose of the objectives becomes obvious.

Training has been covered in a previous chapter, but its use of objectives is worth discussing again. Training is the key to consistency. Objectives are like stairs in a multi-level building. Each objective accomplished is one more stair toward completion, so after a full training program, whether in a probationary period or in a regular job setting, the objectives allow someone to see that he made it past each step in order to get to the next level.

Even if you do not want to implement a full action plan, document short- and long-term objectives. By documenting short- and long-term objectives, you will find that more will be accomplished in a timely manner, no matter how large or small a project is. This is what is what using implementation tools through the means of objectives means.[104]

As a mid-level manager, short term strategies leading to long term achievements will be used quite often, as this is the best method to keep score of goals that are reached. Both upper-level managers and first-level managers will view this score, so use it wisely.

> **Objectives are like stairs in a multi-level building. Each objective accomplished is one more stair toward completion...**

CHAPTER 30
ASSESSMENT

1. **Writing them down is the hardest part of setting goals, but what do you do with them then?** You implement a plan using objectives.

2. **Are all objectives met in one step?** Goals may be short-term, completed promptly, but longer-term objectives take more time and may be a series of short-term goals put together.

3. **Why does it pay to use short-term objectives?** An individual or a group will have a feeling of accomplishment when they meet short-term objectives. This helps keep the motivation going in a positive direction.

CHAPTER CHALLENGE

As seen in this chapter, not all goals/objectives need to be in the professional arena. List a non-professional goal that you would like to achieve.

31

ECONOMICS:
The Root of All Evil

" *Economics is sometimes associated with the study and defense of selfishness and material inequality, but it has an egalitarian and civil libertarian core that should be celebrated.* — Tyler Cowen "

CHAPTER PREVIEW

1

The media tends to make it sound bad that companies make a profit, but that is economics.

2

Companies need accountants, and managers need to know what accounting is doing for the company.

3

Business has many programs within its structure that require knowledge of economics.

When starting our family, my wife and I decided to build our dream house. This turned out to be an arduous lesson in economics. We had a plan, a budget, and the foresight to see our dream come true. We first set our goal. Then we put together a financial plan, which became the basis for a budget. After this was completed, we had to find a qualified builder. The final phase was to agree on a contract.

Eight months later, we moved into our new house. We were fortunate that (for the most part) everything went as planned. Planning and knowing where the money went was critical. One month after signing the contract to build our house, Hurricane Hugo struck the United States. This caused the cost of raw materials to increase by an average of 25 percent. We were economically lucky.

Good or bad, economics determines the viability of any business, and economics becomes that much more critical as you work your way up the corporate ladder. Mid-level managers are now being fed economic numbers from upper management and are expected to achieve the company's economic goals, beginning at lower management levels. This is not an easy task. The question then becomes, *do managers need knowledge of accounting?*

> **Good or bad, economics determines the viability of any business...**

As stated earlier, a manager is *somebody who is responsible for directing and controlling the work and staff of a business, or of a department within it.*[41] In order to control a business, a manager must know all aspects of the business that affect the manager's area. This may involve production, sales and marketing, inventory control, finance, personnel, and salaries, as well as other items.

Two points that managers must keep a close eye on are personnel and money. Managers do need some knowledge of accounting, but how best to use that knowledge is sometimes not readily perceptible. For example, production managers have a language of their own that deals directly with the production of products for given customers. This language may include production terms, engineering tools, or machinery instructions.

Likewise, accounting has its own unique terms and language. This language difference may constitute a roadblock for managers. However, managers learn that accounting is useful in performing their job, saving time, and for making the correct financial decisions on a day-to-day basis.

One reason that businesses fail is if the people in charge do not know what is going on with the company's money. Granted, some businesses fail because of circumstances beyond their control, especially in a bad economy. However, generally speaking, when a company fails it is due to a lack of funds.

To avoid this problem, managers should be familiar with the organization's information systems, which consist of formal programs like payroll and purchasing and informal agendas (like the grapevine) that lead to impressions and opinions.

Furthermore, managers need to understand the company's internal accounting system.[143] An automobile may be driven without a gas gauge, but sometimes the driver may run out of gas or spend excessive time filling the gas tank. The same holds true for a manager who does not use the company's accounting program. A manager must know where the company is making, losing, and paying its money. If the manager does not know where the money is going, the company will run out of it.

Production, retail, and service businesses have changed dramatically over the last ten years. These changes have affected all areas of business, including managing and accounting. Some changes that require managerial attention include:

1. **Just-in-time:** Companies do not want to hold any extra inventory, as extra inventory costs the company money.

2. **Raw material inventory control:** Most organizations closely monitor their raw material inventory because this equates to money.

3. **Production cells:** Companies are focusing more and more on production labor, as labor itself is a known cost, but how to get more out of that known cost equates to production improvements that affect the bottom line.

4. **Natural resources:** As of late, organizations are focused on two areas related to natural resources. One is being *green*, using as few natural resources as possible, while the other is the cost of energy as a whole.

5. **Lean:** This is a way to bring all activities together to verify that the least amount of energy is used to order, schedule, produce products, and ship the product out the door.

The concept may be easy to master, but the discipline necessary to do it is not. One common illustration of what Lean means is to *handle a piece of paper once.* Try doing this for a day, it is more difficult than it sounds.

Also, try to follow a path called Value Stream Mapping,[70] which is the process of recording the path, steps, or flow of paperwork within a given time period (a day, a week, or a month), to see how often one action is repeated, thereby wasting time.

One might follow how purchase orders are entered into a company's system. After a while, if plotted on a map, one thin line would show one action. After one week, that thin line may become a heavy, thick line in the areas in which Lean action needs to be taken. Thick lines means that time has been wasted.

As highlighted by the above points, a relationship between production managers and accounting does exist. In order for a manager to understand how a business runs, he must understand not only the physical functions of an organization but the financial functions as well. He must know the accounting system, costs, and charges in order to make faster and more informed decisions. In addition to the above, managers must recognize these concepts:

1. **Just-in-time:** Keeping inventories low may cost money, such as when there is a low-volume production run with increased labor setup. Managers may not focus on bottom-line production costs if the Just-in-Time system seems to be working. An accounting department should have historical data to compare inventories to production labor costs.

2. **Raw material inventory control:** It is easy to say, *keep raw materials, stocks, and supply inventories low*, but what are the costs of running out of materials and paying extra to get the materials in order to maintain production schedules? There may also be increased labor costs to make up for late materials.

    Material costs themselves may fluctuate, so purchase timing is critical. An accounting department would have numbers that could be reviewed in this regard.

3. **Production cells:** Managers should know what costs are being generated by production, but in order to set up production cells or customer service centers, there might be conflicts with capitalization of new equipment in designing a functional cell. An accounting department would have information about capitalization breakdowns.

4. **Natural resources:** This is a relatively new area of business for managers. Being *green* costs money. Payback for energy improvements tends to be in long-term investments.

    The question again relates to capitalization versus return on investment, and normally this involves some detailed accounting numbers. Without assistance or records from accounting, managers will have to guess.[143]

5. **Lean:** As stated earlier, Lean is a discipline. The first exercise is to map out steps taken by all personnel (Value Stream Mapping). Look for overlaps, and determine why they exist and what may be done to prevent them. Lean is designed to eliminate waste while showing where continuous improvements may be made.[124] Capitalization may also be necessary.

The items listed above are a few examples of how to understand if your business is running optimally. Each business has its own program for controlling costs. A manager in today's production world cannot afford errors in the managing of money for his organization. A manager must use all of the tools at his disposal to make the fastest and most accurate decisions regarding money.

To do this, managers must become part-time accountants. Managers must understand the financial path of an organization in order to avoid losses and assist in financial improvements. The lack of this knowledge affects the company's profit margins first and foremost, so if a manager is to be of value, she needs accounting information, and she needs to know how to use it.

As mentioned earlier, where money is involved, extra precaution must be taken for two reasons. First, money gives people a reason to steal, and second, a system must have checks and balances so that everyone knows that the business is being run honestly.

Some basic programs in finance help with accountability. Responsibility Accounting breaks down costs by the use of centers: Costs, Profit, Investment, Economic Value Added, and Controllability Principle in this manner:

1. **Costs:** inputs through labor, materials, and supplies.

2. **Profit:** input mix, product mix, and selling prices (output).

3. **Investment:** input mix, product mix, selling prices (output), and capital investment in each group.

4. **Economic Value Added:** what is done in a process or function that adds to the value of what is being made or sold.

5. **Controllability Principle:** controlled costs are controlled by the affected manager, whereas the uncontrolled costs are not controlled by the affected manager.[143]

This list includes areas of business accounting that pinpoint where cost numbers are generated, controlled, and audited. However, this is not the area where the costs are recorded and paid. While the responsible manager may have some limited control, once the records go to finance, the manager normally is done with his review unless accounting has a question. This shows that accounting is auditing production, but production normally does not audit accounting, so a different approach is necessary.

Due to bad practices and press awareness in the accounting industry over the last ten years, governments and businesses have introduced checks and double checks. Regulators from government agencies, such as the Securities and Exchange Commission, Financial Accounting Standards Board, and the Internal Revenue Service have all taken a closer look at what companies are doing with their money. Methods that companies tend to follow to support their financial numbers and use to report to the government or shareholders include:

1. Provide information necessary to identify the most profitable product or service and the pricing used to achieve the desired volume.

2. Provide information to detect production inefficiencies to ensure that the proposed product and volumes are produced at the lowest costs.

3. When combined with performance evaluation and rewards, offer incentives for managers to maximize firm value.

4. Support the financial accounting and tax accounting reporting functions.

5. Contribute more to the firm's value than to costs.[143]

When costs are reported in the proper manner, production/retail/customer service centers and accounting departments will be able to explain where the numbers were generated and how they are used to support management decisions.

CHAPTER 31
ASSESSMENT

1. **Whether you are a Republican or a Democrat, economics is not a sin to talk about. Why?** If a business does not know the amount of money that it is generating and spending, it will go out of business. The business must also understand how to improve those figures because the competition is already doing this. It is not wrong to make a profit because profits are used to build and improve a business. Remember, no profits equals no business.

2. **Do business economics involve employees?** Employees are a big piece of the puzzle but not the only piece. Raw materials, equipment, and the environment all play a role in the bottom line.

3. **Because money is involved, should we assume that everyone is honest?** The opposite is true. Because money is involved, audits must be performed to make sure that everyone is honest.

CHAPTER CHALLENGE

If you were to start a business today, how would you prioritize your economic needs and why?

32

UNKNOWN EXTERNAL FACTORS

There's always going to be the circumstances you can't plan for. There's always the unexpected relevance and the serendipity. — Jason Silva

CHAPTER PREVIEW

1

A single business cannot control everything.

2

Plan on outside people, companies, or events to mess things up.

3

Be flexible to adjust to any situation that arises.

T*he best laid plans of mice and men often go awry* is a line from a poem written by Robert Burns in 1785.[138] These words have meaning in management. No matter how carefully a project is planned, even though we plan to the best of our abilities, something may still go wrong.[138]

Any manager who thinks that he has total control is a fool and does not understand what Robert Burns was saying. A manager looks forward to see if there may be problems ahead. A dynamite manager adjusts when problems arise that are out of his control. Internal factors should be seen ahead of time so that a manager may try to prevent problems before they occur. Many problems might be accounted for by using the material from previous chapters of this book, but external factors are more difficult to see.

At 15 years old, someone in my high school class bullied me. I tried to avoid this person as much as possible. While at school I was able to use the building, the teachers, and the other students as a buffer and to control to some degree any confrontations that took place on school grounds.

But one day that changed. The problem intensified when this person waited for me a block away from the high school. I had to decide whether to avoid him, which was unlikely, or to tackle the conflict right then and there. I chose to address the problem once and for all. He and I exchanged some words, but in the end, we were able to work things out. Luckily for me, the truce held throughout the rest of our high school days.

You do not always have control, so you must plan for external factors to wreak havoc

> **A dynamite manager adjusts when problems arise that are out of his control.**

on your business. Different types of plans will briefly be explained below so that you may see what a threat or a concern looks like. To be aware of a potential risk, however, a detailed investigation must be conducted. These investigations should be timely.

These external factors, which may change over time, are broken down into three groups:

1. **Remote environment:**

   A. **Economic:** One external concern might be with an outside entity that may affect money values, such as the European Economic Community (EEC).

   B. **Social:** Changes or shifts with people outside the work environment may affect working conditions, like flexible work weeks, lump-sum vacation plans, increasing diversity in labor markets, and as of late, delayed retirement in labor positions.

   C. **Political:** These factors involve legal and regulatory limits, which may include minimum wage, antitrust laws, fair-trade, pollution, pricing within government markets, and other labor laws.

   D. **Technological:** As a manager, you must be aware of the changing world, the most notable change being the Internet. Companies that saw the real benefits of this new breakthrough jumped on building websites to promote their businesses within a newly existing and rapidly growing market.

   E. **Ecological:** There must be concerns about how a company handles its impact on the environment as well as how outsiders view how it handles that impact. Water and air pollution are areas in which the government has stepped up surveillance of companies, so management must stay on top of these matters.

2. **Industry environment:**

   A. Entry barriers: This is the first bridge that a company must cross if it wishes to enter into a new area of business. Some typical barriers include the cost of money to break into the new business, product differentiation that makes your product better, access to distribute into the new market, and government policies.

B. Powerful suppliers: When a supplier becomes strong, it may raise prices when it wants to if it is operating in a market that has limited suppliers. One example of this would be a soft drink concentrate supplier to a bottler. The market dictates pricing to the bottler, but its supplier may not care.

C. Powerful buyers: Walmart buyers tell its suppliers that if they want the business, this is the price that Walmart is willing to pay. MasterCard charges merchants a certain percentage of each sale when a customer uses their card. If the business wants to make sales, it agrees to pay.

D. Substitute products: Just because you think that your product is the best, this may mean nothing to a customer. If a different product may take the place of yours and is less expensive, you will lose. This happened with sugar and sugar substitutes, but it may happen with any product in the marketplace.

E. Competitive rivalry: This is seen quite often in marketing with pricing competition, introduction of new products, or price-cutting. Home improvement stores cut prices and make new product announcements weekly. The automotive business uses price-cutting events to advertise new and improved products.

3. **Operating environment:**

A. Competitors: In some markets, keeping up with competitors is a full-time job. It involves knowing market share, pricing competitiveness, facilities location, raw material costs in the market, and caliber of personnel. You must know where you stand in relation to all competitors.

B. Credit: Because business is not always stable, it pays to have reliable banking support to assist in times of need, for possible short-term loans.

C. Customers: This is the most vulnerable area of business, as it is difficult to know a company's position with its customers. A collection of factors play into a buyer's decision to buy, such as location of the store, demographics, psychographics, and buyer behavior. To complicate matters, consumers' attitudes are a never-ending change, and this is where public relations is critical.

D. Suppliers: As seen earlier, a company must know its suppliers. A supplier may cause trouble when it comes to pricing and delivery. A company must know that the price quoted is fair to the market, that the supplier will deliver, and that all charges, such as shipping, are clear and up-front.

E. Labor: This may become a business-ending problem. Regardless of whether unionized, all things labor must be fair in the market in which it is found. If it is not, workers could strike or slow work down. This does not mean that businesses should lie down and pay whatever people want, but the overall market will dictate labor value.

   One example of this is the toy market. Most toys are made in China because of the cheap labor. United States labor is too high, so the choices are to reduce labor costs, increase production, or combine both. This is what markets in the U.S. are doing presently.[104]

What companies sell or market will affect which of the above points a company needs to focus on, and some of them will need constant surveillance. But even small companies must be aware of all of the above points if they are to stay in business for a long time.

This concern goes across all markets and businesses. Most companies have special groups of employees that watch this area of the business, but a manager still needs to know why and how external factors affect her employer.

CHAPTER 32
ASSESSMENT

1. **Small- to medium-sized businesses tend to do poorly with external concerns. Why?** Managers of small businesses concern themselves more with day-to-day operations and do not watch outside changes.

2. **What three business environments should a manager be aware of?** Remote, Industry, and Operating

3. **In order to be on top of the never-ending external changes that may take place, should a company have one person looking out for the whole organization?** More than one person should keep an eye on external factors that may affect a business because at least three different aspects of the business are involved.

CHAPTER CHALLENGE

Name some external concerns that the USA might have and why?

CASE STUDY 6

COMPANY CULTURE

CASE GOALS

1	**2**	**3**
A lot of activities may be going on underground in a large company. Be aware of all	Culture takes multiple different forms within a company.	Cultures, as do people, change over time.

When a manager is working his way up the ladder, he becomes more involved in how the company is run and how it will be run in the future. In this Case Study, we will review Magna International Inc. to see why leadership and culture are important to an organization that has had sales of more than $26 billion. We have been exploring leadership throughout this book, but we need to better explain culture before we go any further.

Culture is the feeling within a company and how management is able to control how it operates, communicates, and directs both short- and long-term goals.

Multiple cultures exist within an organization, but executive management culture is the backbone of the company. Mid-level managers also have their own culture, but it must fit within the executive management culture, or it will not work.

As you will see below, it will be easy to recognize a culture or cultures that you have witnessed before. Managers need to find the one culture that works for them and that fits with executive management, however, over time (and through promotions), this culture may change, so managers need to study all cultures because they never know which one they will be immersed in next.

This Case Study details the various cultures and the question of why a mid-level manager should understand this topic. By reviewing this information, a mid-level manager will see how an organization may be built and also understand how her present employer decided years before how to structure the company.

By knowing what cultures exist, a mid-level manager may then determine if the system is still holding the value that it was designed to hold or if it needs updating, in which case the mid-level manager may state her case to executives. Executives should be open to questions concerning the company's culture. Executives should keep a pulse on the entire company culture, and this leads us to our Case Study.

Frank Stronach started what is now Magna International Inc. in 1957 in Toronto, Canada, from a one-man plant, and he and his employees and managers have been able to build a customer- and goal-driven organization.[81]

Organizational culture is generally broken down into sections and subsections. The sections and sub-sections make it easier to determine which parts of the organization comply with all of the requirements of the organization and which areas do not. Generally a business will choose one type of culture and stay with it, but you will see that Magna believed in and followed a multiple-culture approach. There are different ways to break company culture down, but the ones used in this review are as follows:

1. Clan

2. Adhocracy

3. Market

4. Hierarchy

Within each culture is a set of sub-cultures:

A. Leader type

B. Value drivers

C. Theory of effectiveness

D. Quality improvement strategy[100]

When using this format, it becomes easier to discern if an organization is being held together by loyalty and tradition with the emphasis on long-term human resource development in order to reduce personnel conflicts.[100] Along with the above approach, a combination of strategic organizational requirements is necessary to permit a comparison.[88]

Frank Stronach started small, but it did not take long before his company expanded. Back in 1957, when the business was known as Multimatic, it would have been hard to say whether he had a strategic plan or an organizational culture in mind, but in the following years, it was plain that he at least had a vision. By 1969, Multimatic had merged with Magna Electronics, which was a publicly traded aerospace, defense, and industrial component manufacturing company. Sales that year were $4.5 million, and so the corporate culture emerged.

In 1972, Magna opened its first U.S. plant in Iowa, and its annual sales jumped to $8.5 million.[81] In 1973, Magna changed its name to Magna International Inc. and finished the year with sales of $15.5 million. In 2010, Magna announced its conception of an electric vehicle and became the foremost automotive parts supplier in North America, with annual sales of $23.7 billion.[81]

Growing as Magna has, it had to operate under multiple organizational cultures from scratch. As Magna grew the culture changed. Magna began as a clan culture and then moved into a market culture, which allowed more freedom to explore, expand, and re-define, including its HR functions.[88]

Magna was not afraid to move in more than one direction to improve its position to not only support the automotive market but also to become the key player in the automotive supply chain. Magna did not limit its expertise to components; it boasted business savvy by maintaining separate business groups. Each group, whether privatized or traded on the public market, had to generate its own profits, and all employees were given a share of those profits.

This built a proactive, positive attitude among employees that promoted continued advancements in the automotive business and enabled Magna to become the largest supplier and innovator in the automotive supply chain.[81] The apparent business-minded attitude under which Magna operates explains why it has been as successful as it has.[81]

Clan Culture

One definition of the word clan means the process of getting people together to mutually work toward a common goal.[51] With Magna, it meant group-building by a team leader, which was a practice at Magna in the late 1980s.

Magna's human resources management attempted to implement improved production and alternate models of handling personnel interactions. The attempt was modeled after Total Quality Management, kaizen (an early Japanese philosophy of Lean and continuous improvement), and Just-in-Time in an effort to avoid unionization.[136] Conflicts between personnel and management came down to poor communications.[136] HR was able to avoid unionization up until 2010, but its hands were tied because corporate management had a dictator-type mentality.

The clan culture became a *class-based superiority of management to the shop floor personnel*, which meant that corporate management was exceptionally domineering.[136]

The above-mentioned programs placed the emphasis on corporate culture, led to improved communications with all personnel, management-directed work teams, contingent pay, individualized career development, and industrial relations similar to union environments. With the above practices, Magna controlled its labor, as each division was sized reasonably to maintain control.[136] For a limited time, human resources was able to contain and improve on an employee clan culture, but the focus was still heavily corporate with limited selling points enticing to individuals.

Years later, at least one division of Magna has become unionized.[25] Based on Magna's history, the same focus that helped Magna thrive was also at the heart of its management versus employee disputes, an aggressive approach to business. HR was able to mitigate the hostile environment somewhat, but it could not stop corporate management who took advantage of Canadian laws to further their own advancement.[136]

If human resources had represented the individual worker a bit better, it may have saved time and headaches. This deficiency caused the organizational culture to suffer, but all was not lost.

Adhocracy Culture

A culture better suited for Magna was adhocracy. An adhocracy culture is forged with a potent working environment.[100] As seen by some of Magna's business ventures, Magna's management group, along with its employees, was encouraged to take risks in order to make advancements. In Magna's Employee charter, HR set the tone of the business with the statement, *At the heart of our operating structure is an entrepreneurial culture.*[79] This statement was proclaimed by Magna's CEO and progressed downward through management and human resources by establishing operating philosophies.[79]

To encourage an entrepreneurial culture as a more enjoyable way of life, Magna's CEO instituted an employee profit sharing program in 1975. This program was called the Employee Equity and Profit Participation Plan.[81] The driving force behind this plan was that the CEO wanted all employees to buy into innovation, advancement, and progressive thinking, which also became part of the Employee Charter, and this became HR's attempt to encourage all employees to build on innovation.[79] Shortly after this program began, Magna moved into the Clan Culture of the 1980s.

Magna has had no problem being innovative, looking into the future, and using new resources effectively.[88] Because of Magna's forward thinking, it instituted new quality standards by developing new principles about how to conduct business with automotive manufacturers by containing all facets of production needed to build automobiles.

Though it started small, Magna grew quickly, and HR had to grow as well.[81] However, because of Magna's rapid growth and merging divisions, the human resources department became segregated, which led to confusion, especially at the shop floor level.

Subsequently, Magna's HR department had to regroup, and in 1984, it tried to mend past mistakes by introducing a new corporate constitution and rights to the employees' profit sharing program, which did improve conditions for a short time.[136] Magna's HR team was on the right track but did not go far enough because shop floor employees still felt that day-to-day income and conditions were lagging behind other similar manufacturing groups and that Magna was taking advantage of labor conditions.[136]

Corporate HR should have been able to comprehend this point of frustration with the employees. While the business, sales, and engineering segments of the corporation read their clients well, HR fell short of its responsibilities.[88]

Market Culture

Market-based mentality is where Magna excelled. When reviewing Magna's history, it is evident that what Magna has accomplished since its inception in 1957 is extraordinary. It is apparent that Magna is a goal-driven organization based on its growth. If Magna was not buying companies, it was merging, spinning off companies not part of the future core business, or promoting new products, which were all part of its central goal of becoming the most dominant supplier for all automobile manufacturers, which became a fact in 2008.[81]

Aggressive action was the basis of the corporate attitude, and again, all areas excelled except human resources. Because the corporate culture dictated that each division was on its own, corporate let each division handle its own HR responsibilities. In some cases it worked, but in others it did not.

A prime example was Magna's Windsor, Ontario, plant, which became unionized because of fears related to management.[80] Magna, including its HR department, focused on its customers and did an impressive job, but more attention should have been paid to Magna's employees' welfare. Magna's foundation was always customer-driven, and Magna was constantly measuring its customers' needs, wants, and dislikes, which helped corporate strategies.[122]

Interestingly, in Magna's financial reports for 2009, an increase in funding for a new electric vehicle and charity contributions were shown, but the company's profit sharing program showed reductions not increases. Did HR anticipate this turn of events, and was it handled correctly?[122]

Human resources should have anticipated that some negative impact would result as part of the Key Performance Indicators. This is where all employees' input to improve the company and profits are recognized with monetary acknowledgment for all employees, but when profits were posted the indicators were not recognized to improve profits. Because money from the company went into other areas of business, money did not go into an individual's account. HR should have understood that an individual's pay and benefits are significant to that individual.[88]

The defining concepts in the market culture are measuring client preferences, productivity, new external partnerships to benefit the organization, increasing competitiveness, and involving customers and suppliers for overall customer satisfaction.[100] Magna has done well in the above area, but all of its work almost went for naught in 2001.

Magna was involved in a novel venture with Lincoln Mercury on a new project called the Blackwood.[84] Magna failed to measure the difficulty that it would have making some of the key components for this new vehicle and missed some delivery dates, which led to an upset customer, which, in turn, led to missed sales from end users.

The debacle intensified when Mercury's corporate owners, Ford Motor Company, withheld payments to Magna. In one swift move, Magna violated all rules: service the market and the customer before all else, and do not let a customer down within the marketculture.[100] Over the next several years, Magna was able to regroup with the Ford Motor Company, primarily because of its strong hierarchy culture.[81]

Hierarchy Culture

Magna's success has been due largely to its hierarchy culture, which means a formalized, structured work environment that is proud of efficiency-based coordination and organization.[100] Due to Magna's growth, Magna used more than one culture over time. However, the hierarchy culture was in place from day one because of the president of the company. Magna has been able to improve its efficiency in building and supporting the automobile manufacturing market. All leading automotive manufacturers now rely heavily on Magna for key parts and assemblies.[81]

This progress happened over time with well-defined, efficient, and effective controls. With quality and procedure requirements such as ISO 9000 and TS 16949 in the automotive business, items such as error detection, process controls, problem-solving, and quality tools are mandatory. Its competence as an automotive supplier requires that all quality parameters be met on an daily basis, so Magna's continued success shows that it has a strong hierarchy culture.[21]

The human resources side of Magna's hierarchy culture has been weak. There have been numerous attempts to bond all of Magna's employees, and to some degree it has worked, as each division has its own goals, but one set of corporate goals exists within the Employee Charter and the Magna International Constitution.[79]

The high points of the Employee Charter include a fair enterprise culture, job security while finding the best way to produce at the least expense, safe working conditions, fair treatment for opportunities of individual qualification and performance, competitive wages and benefits, employee equity and profit participation, an improved communication and information system, an employee relations advisory board, and a hotline to call to voice concerns and opinions.[79]

Magna has shown that it is a power to be reckoned with. Beginning as a startup company in 1957 and growing to a multi-directional company with $23.7 billion in sales in 2010, Magna must have consistently been doing something right. However, from an organizational culture standpoint, Magna stood out. Over time Magna has been able to adjust for growth and variations in business. Magna has adopted all four cultures but stayed with two primary cultures. On occasion Magna has embraced two cultures at one time, but only due to the company's size.

Magna built numerous cultures and utilized innovation, took risks, anticipated customer needs, maintained its vision, made market share its first priority, and kept cost controls in mind at all times.[100] The above points would be included in the adhocracy, market, and hierarchy cultures, and again, Magna did an excellent job in these areas. But as far as the clan culture goes, Magna had difficulties, and this is why this culture was used widely by itself or with other cultures.[100] Magna did indeed have strong management, but this was also the negative side of the clan culture.

Magna's former CEO, Frank Stronach, was so dedicated to viewing the company's goals and its customers that its employees did not always get a fair deal. This is not to say that the employees were treated any worse than any other automotive business employee, they were not, but corporate human resources should have con-

> **A manager must choose the right culture that fits the future plans of an organization and the personnel within it.**

centrated more on employee pay and benefits and making the employees happy.[136]

Human resources took a lot of correct steps to improve communications via its hotline, employee relations advisory board, and manufacturing teams, but in the big picture, and what led to the unionization of one plant (so far, were issues with wages and job security, among other things.

The actual agreement in the union's first collective bargaining agreement with Magna was a $3.00 an hour wage increase and layoff and job security protection as well as other benefits, so the writing was on the wall, and Magna's HR group either failed to makes its point, or it was not listening when plant employees voiced their opinions and concerns during a lengthy time prior to the unionization vote.[25,88] In either case, it is now going to cost Magna more to do business.

Magna has seen what happens when corporate management and HR do not listen and react to numerous failures, as with an unhappy labor force. One possible stumbling block may now be out of the way because as of May 5, 2011, Frank Stronach has stepped down as Chairman of the Board. Frank Stronach certainly contributed to Magna's overall success, but it also appears that he had many opportunities to address employee concerns and did not.

As David Tyerman, Canaccord Genuity analyst, said concerning Frank Stronach, *the shareholders will be better off without him.*[33]

One thing is for sure, Stronach built a sterling organization. Today's business climate may not fit the likings of a Frank Stronach, but without his vision and drive, through various company purchases, mergers, and innovations, Magna would not have been able to achieve such phenomenal success.[81] A manager must choose the right culture that fits the future plans of an organization and the personnel within it.

Again, this decision is not set in stone. Upper management and the Board of Directors should examine the state of the business as it is periodically and review whether a culture change is needed. That is why a manager must be aware of what is happening not only in his business, but also in the environment around him, including his competitors.

CASE STUDY 6
ASSESSMENT

1. **Does a front-line manager have any effect on culture?** To change the overall culture of a company, the front-line manager has limited input, but understanding how cultures work allows a manager to more easily understand where she fits in and how she may help a culture to work.

2. **Do all cultures work the same way?** No. The management style that a company chooses must match how a company is to run. Not all cultures are effective with every management type. If you want to have a market culture but manage in the hierarchy culture style, there will be a disconnect between the customer and commands from upper management.

3. **Do cultures change?** Cultures may change and tend to do so when businesses are bought or change hands. This is often seen when different family members take over a company. One individual may be in favor of a hierarchy culture to begin with, but when a new family member gets involved, it may change to a clan culture.

CASE CHALLENGE

Choose a company and write about which type of culture is present and why it does or does not work.

33

CHAIN OF COMMAND

Like a good parent can't also be his child's best friend, a leader with authority requires some separation from subordinates. — Simon Sinek

CHAPTER PREVIEW

1

Know the links of your chain.

2

A too long chain is unproductive.

3

A firm chain equals thorough communications.

One thing that new managers normally have trouble adjusting to is the chain of command. New managers want to flaunt their authority and tend to over-reach their assigned boundaries, which may get them into trouble. After some lessons, though, new managers learn to follow the organizational chart.

In this chapter, the chain of command takes on two different meanings. The manager must know who he is supposed to report to and why, but company executives must also evaluate if all levels are effective. This maintains better communications. Executives must constantly review the corporate structure to verify that all levels of management are needed.[65]

General Motors (GM) may serve as an example in this regard. Back in the late 1980s, Professor Peter Drucker, an Austrian-born American management consultant, educator, and author, who invented the concept known as management by objectives,[139] wrote an article that focused on GM's incompetent management.[91] During this time, GM had fifty-two levels of management. The primary duty of each level of management was to protect the level above it, known as protecting the hierarchy of management.[91]

This only works for so long, as may be seen with GM. Management levels were drastically reduced from 1990 to 2005.

As Professor Drucker stated back in 1987, GM could cut half of its management levels and not even notice that they were missing.[91] Ultimately, this is what GM was forced to do to stay in business (along with a government bailout).

AT&T did not wait for the economy to steer it in the correct direction. The AT&T breakup led to employment reductions, while at the same time the company adjusted to new competitors reducing its overall market share.[106]

Why be concerned with multiple levels of management within the chain of command? The first reason is costs, because management, especially at upper levels, is not cheap, so a company may pour money into management that basically produces nothing. The chain of command may be correct, but the cost and control is as important, and this was the case with GM. The cost outweighed the output.

GM did not begin with fifty-two levels of management. It grew out of control, which was another problem. As W. Edwards Deming has stated, 85 percent of company failures are a function of management.[31]

With a single level of management, messages or instructions have are liable chance of being understood, however, with fifty-two levels of management, there is little chance that a message that trickles down from top management to lower levels of management and employees will be error-free.

> **Managers must review and keep only the information that pertains to their level of management.**

As mentioned earlier, another factor that compounds problems with the chain of command is The Peter Principle. Getting the message through various levels of management is difficult enough, but with added layers of incompetent managers, those promoted beyond their abilities, this becomes a multi-dimensional problem because managers may hide within the organization and never be found.

In a multi-level organization, proper communications have a slim chance of getting to the lower levels accurately.[73] Managers must review and keep only the information that pertains to their level of management. This allows the most transparent message to make its way to personnel so that the entire business is well run.

Determining whether each level in the chain of command is critical is ultimately up to owners and stockholders. Stockholders of the company steer the company to make money because stockholders own a piece of the company through the purchase of stocks. If a company does not make money, the stockholders sell their stocks, and the company does not stay in business.

As of late, this economic fact has come under fire because of greedy management, as with the JPMorgan mortgage scandal.[86] JPMorgan was irresponsible, but basic economic principles state that if the balance sheet does not show a profit, a company is doomed. That being said, stockholders do have a responsibility to the company and society. Stockholders should be aware of how information and policies flow through all levels of management, if the organization is to operate at its fullest potential.

General Motors was an example of a poorly run organization from the top down, but another GM, General Mills, is a fine example of a well-run company. By looking at General Mills, we will see illustrations that show how the chain of command is supposed to be maintained throughout an organization.

CHAPTER 33
ASSESSMENT

1. **Why should we understand the chain of command?** As in the military, one may not maintain order if a private is telling the commander what to do.

2. **How is the best way for a company to communicate?** Communication paths follow the chain of command, so that all messages get to the proper personnel.

3. **If the chain of command is not followed, what happens?** Top management may get upset if information does not get to where it is needed because the communication path goes in both directions, top-down and bottom-up.

CHAPTER CHALLENGE

Find and write about a company that communicates well or that does a poor job of communicating and why you believe this to be the case.

GENERAL MILLS

CASE GOALS

1	2	3
It is not easy to maintain an enormous organization's culture.	Communications must be driven.	Make expectations clear to help motivate others.

General Mills is a marketing-driven company with strong leadership; a complex, hierarchical structure; and a variety of business units. The first order of business is that executives understand that the company must please the everyday person.[47] As such, the company promotes talented and committed people.

General Mills insists that its employees learn, grow, and contribute to the community. It also believes in innovation via the ideas of employees. All of these activities support delivering outstanding performance and quality products.[47]

The first step in establishing the chain of command is to determine the code of conduct for everyone in the organization. This assists in making

> **Communication to all employees must be consistent and clear. Employees must also understand how they are to act.**

clear what the stakeholders (someone who owns a piece of the business and under some circumstances is allowed to hear about what the company is doing and plans on doing) vote into place for future conduct requirements. It should also determine how all employees will handle themselves throughout the organization. This shows employees where the organization will offer support, such as educational assistance, assistance for working mothers, and cancer awareness, which is what General Mills has done.[46,47]

General Mills' stakeholders must be accountable to all employees, so General Mills has hired a diverse group of individuals who have integrity. This group must deliver superior performance and exceptional return on investment that may be seen by investors and the community around each company location.[47] This is a tall order, but General Mills has reached its goal, and the main reason is that each level of management knows what the chain of command means.

General Mills maintains continuity through its human resources groups. Human resources is centralized, meaning that communication branches out to different divisions from one central point and maintains a direct connection to corporate while also maintaining a relationship with each business unit with which it works.[66]

Sales does not work closely with marketing. Marketing functions are driven by a philosophy of brand management in which executives work across product lines.[46] Dedicated teams concentrate on individual customers by way of strong contact with corporate. This allows General Mills to service its customers in a way that best fits its customers' business models.[8,63]

It also allows certain General Mills groups to see what corporate is directing, while at the same time personnel may see what their customers are asking for. However, additional methods are used to communicate the company's needs. Employees are always the bottom line. Every employee receives an annual performance review that includes the setting of goals and objectives and an individual development plan. If an employee under-performs, the employee receives a performance improvement plan, and if that does not work, disciplinary action is taken.[8]

General Mills is creating an environment in which business success comes when employees feel empowered to take initiative, voice their opinions, and build on their experiences within the company and the community[47]

General Mills goes one step further by writing and publishing a code of conduct, presenting its position on social responsibilities. General Mills' employees get involved with volunteer activities for the environment, wellness, improved product labeling, cancer research, school donations, and other social causes.[46] These activities, communications, and reviews come down to one point. General Mills' employees realize that they cannot sit around and enjoy themselves because their competition is keeping up with new products and technology.

What does all of this mean to a new manager? General Mills has put into place programs that a new manager must implement or enforce in order maintain continuity. A new manager must understand the message from upper management. If the message is not understood, the manager must ask for clarification. Communication to all employees must be consistent and clear. Employees must also understand how they are to act.

A code of conduct is a tool that may be used to verify that all personnel get the same message. To confirm that all elements of the code of conduct are understood, reviews and action plans must be set up at certain frequencies when personnel do not meet minimum expectations. This protocol must be maintained and enforced, or it will not work. General Mills performs all of these essentials, and its employees know what is expected, but also they understand what it will take to get promoted.[47]

CASE STUDY 7
ASSESSMENT

1. **Why does the chain of command at General Mills work so well?**
   Communication is easily received and understood by all. Communication through the master corporate plan allows the same information to flow downward to individuals and/or groups without loss.

2. **What additional element does General Mills add to its program?**
   General Mills expects its employees, no matter at what level, to get involved with social causes, and the benefits of this are evident.

CASE CHALLENGE

Review the General Mills code of conduct, found on its website at www.generalmills.com, to find a potential weakness and explain why it is a weakness.

PART IV

OUTSIDE CONTRIBUTIONS NEEDED

MAVERICK OF SALES

CASE GOALS

1	2	3
Thinking outside the box may be a tremendous thing.	A SWOT proves to be a useful tool.	Using social media may be beneficial as well.

Hoover's, a company that reviews and publishes profiles of businesses and organizations, declared Southwest Airlines the maverick of the airlines business. In a number of cases, the traditional methods of running an airline have been re-written because of Southwest's approach, including ticket sales, assigned seating, and even the way that airplanes are painted.[58]

Southwest has forced a number of other airlines to re-examine their own business plans by looking deep into how business was done in the past and asking why. It sets aggressive goals and utilizes different advertising theories and overall growth and profit plans.

To determine whether Southwest has accomplished its marketing goals, its SWOT analysis must be reviewed.[69] In brief, Southwest's SWOT looks like this:

1. **Strengths:** high capacity, low price, diverse upper management, increased revenue, domination of short-run flights, profitable.

2. **Weaknesses:** no international flights, no assigned seating, dependent on single producer, lack of travel agent contacts, five organized groups of labor (example: repair mechanics), flight attendants are unionized, carry low-volume freight, do not use e-mail chats, no morning flights.

3. **Opportunities:** national and international markets, growth in older generations, industrial research, growth with Hispanic population, new technologies to new products, longer flights, growth of business and leisure travel.

4. **Threats** (Southwest has many): decline of leisure travel due to economy and terrorism; competing online ticket sales; new government add-ons, such as taxes and fees; increased maintenance programs; gas and oil prices; increased restrictions (example: noise); annual security costs.[62]

Based on this brief SWOT, Southwest went out on a limb to build a different environment in which to do business.

The objective goals should send a positive message concerning the organization to employees and those in the community. Southwest has sent numerous messages to employees and shareholders over the last thirty-eight years related to goals that the organization wished to accomplish. The company began operations in 1967 as Air Southwest, but it was not until 1973 that the company made a profit, and it has remained profitable ever since.

Southwest's marketing objectives are simple to state: dedication to the highest customer service with warmth, friendliness, individual pride, and company spirit; lowest costs; and on-time schedules. Southwest's strategy was to send a decisive message and belief regarding its goals from top management down.[142]

Southwest has not tried to keep its targeting marketing a secret. It has targeted ages from 25 to 54 as a key demographic since 2001.[26] In 2007, though Southwest maintained its previous desired demographic, it then went after the senior citizen crowd by offering discounts, whereas other airlines did not.[87] The foundation of its business is to target people who are willing to pay affordable prices for on-time transportation.[142]

Southwest was one of the first airlines to invest in and rely heavily on Internet sales, which has been its most favorable selling method. Per Anne Murray, Director of Interactive Marketing, Southwest's Ding program drove in up to 65 percent of Southwest's revenue in 2005, and has averaged more than 70 percent through 2008.[3,115] The Ding program targets people who are willing to be alerted via computer to lower-priced ticket options. It also targets customers who want to become loyal to Southwest.

To add to the Ding program, Southwest has targeted customers who desire a complete package and rewards for buying. Customers who wish to save time may go to Southwest's website and buy an airline ticket and reserve a hotel and a rental car at a lower overall cost and receive reward points for the purchase.

To top this, Southwest offers free flights for referrals, so if four friends buy Southwest tickets, one person gets a free ticket. This goes hand-in-hand with Southwest's other targeted group — vacationers. A number of Southwest's flights target common vacation destinations. To increase ticket purchases to these vacation spots, Southwest started the program where a friend could fly for free. Under certain conditions, a customer could get a second ticket for free to particular vacation destinations.[62] However, to target a certain group, there must be a definitive marketing approach, and this is where Southwest has been revolutionary.

As stated earlier, Southwest has been called a maverick, and that is primarily because of its marketing methods. One interesting innovation (and early risk) was the decision to not allow travel agencies to sell tickets. Southwest knew that to save money it needed to deal directly with the customer. In its early years, Southwest offered free flights on television shows and in contests for relatively low advertising costs. The advent of the Internet and personal computers allowed communication directly from an individual to Southwest, thereby generating opportunities for Southwest to market to individuals and for building loyalty.[142]

Once a customer took a flight on Southwest, it was up to the employees to follow through and showcase the Southwest culture. This was the unique business tactic that originated from upper management that was the basis of the company's success. Employees are informed, trained, and empowered to make decisions, supporting innovative thinking. Employees are encouraged to use individual personalities and be funny to win customers over.

Per Fred Taylor, Senior Manager of Proactive Customer Service Communication, this culture has proven that *employee satisfaction drives customer loyalty.*[120]

Some of Southwest's best outcomes have been derived from the use of catch phrases and employees in its advertisements:

1. **Bags Fly Free:** one ad shows baggage handlers making comments about other airlines' extra baggage charges.

2. **The Low Fare Airline:** employees walk through airports talking about Southwest's pricing.

3. **Wanna Get Away:** features embarrassing situations that make people want to get away fast.

4. **Flight Attendant** (which won *AdWeek's* Best Spots in August 2006): most of its advertisements ended with *you are now free to move about the country.*[58]

Southwest tried and succeeded in using social media by being a trendsetter. Southwest utilized direct Internet sales, a blog, and Twitter. Southwest put in extra effort during natural disasters like Hurricane Katrina. Being part of the California *Find Yourself Here* campaign continued advertising to attract new customers, and marketing to business travelers have been rewarding.

Adding to Southwest's attempts to seek more exposure, it announced an international schedule starting in 2014, after buying its long-time rival, AirTran. In all cases, Southwest examined closely how to get the most impact from media coverage at the lowest cost.[34,56,115,142] Southwest's marketing approach began with its own employees, and then it used media efficiently. Southwest's use of advertising media has re-written the book on the methods by which airlines reach the customer. Early on, Southwest offered free flights to those on game shows, sponsorships, and donations of plane tickets that netted the company additional profits from the exposure.

Not enough may be said about Southwest's use of the Internet. The Ding program was way ahead of its time. Getting people to sign up for newsletters, price reduction alerts, and its own advertising resulted in the generation of 65 percent of Southwest's revenue in 2005. The cost of building and maintaining a website was unheard of back then, though it is now a common practice.

The social media strategies that Southwest has utilized have paid dividends. In addition to sending a distinct message that it cares about people, Southwest is complimented by its own employees, which makes new and present customers feel like winners when using Southwest.[120]

Southwest paid for half of the California *Find Yourself Here* advertising campaign, at a cost of $109,489, seeing a 4.5 percent to 11.5 percent increase in sales annually from 2005 through 2009 with this program.[34]

Southwest has also thrown into the mix a group of colorful aircrafts. While Southwest operates only one type of aircraft, it has allowed a number of planes to be painted with likenesses of the state flag of Florida, Tinker Bell, Slam Dunk One, The Spirit of Hope (Ronald McDonald House), and the Triple Crown One, as well as others. Southwest continues its advertising campaigns with the use of outlets such as television and the Internet to promote the lowest-priced fare, the best employees, the most on-time flights, and increased locations to which it flies.

> **Southwest has implemented different programs over the years that have helped to increase its sales and profitability.**

Southwest has implemented different programs over the years that have helped to increase its sales and profitability. Most other airlines have now adopted those of Southwest's policies that have worked, like increased Internet marketing with alerts, combined sales efforts with hotels and auto rentals, and reward programs.

Business structures and cost-reduction programs have also been reviewed closely by competitors, but the Southwest programs were devised by a unique management team, so recreating them may prove difficult, and the timing may be too late. However, not using travel agencies has not yet been tried by other airlines. The most difficult program for other airlines to reproduce will be the culture in which Southwest's employees work. It would take considerable time for the competition to accomplish something similar.

So how is a Case Study about the marketing endeavors of Southwest Airlines useful to a new manager? First, a new manager who wants to work her way up the corporate ladder needs to know her limits and her competition but also be able to think outside the box.

As discussed earlier, SWOTs are of value to new managers, but we will discuss them in a different light in the next chapter as well. Southwest extensively reviewed its Strengths, Weaknesses, Opportunities, and Threats. So too must a new manager know her departments and business sectors with the same passion. Knowing what her SWOTs are will help a manager be prepared in case something needs to change.

A manager must market herself as well, using any number of means. Making others look bad is a commonly used tactic, but it is not a prudent one, and it makes for long-term difficulties for the manager. The best marketing tool is motivation, not only of the manager's personnel but also of the manager herself, if she wants to maintain an area's high standards.

How do demographics factor into what a manager should do? A manager must focus on individuals for sure, but Southwest used a narrow metric to get the 25–54 age group interested in Southwest. Instead of wasting energy marketing to a broad range of customers, it marketed with intensity to a certain sector of the population to achieve more attention, and it worked.

Later Southwest changed its focus to retired persons and offered discounts. A manager may achieve similar results by concentrating on groups within his area. A manager must be able to tell what groups are in the realm of his responsibility and find out what makes them tick, thus saving time and energy.

Lastly, Southwest began the Ding program as a reward system to draw people back to Southwest. A manager may use a reward program as well. The reward does not have to be cash. Recognition, even by itself, is a strong tool that tends to be overlooked. Promotions may also help determine who cares about an area.

So, as seen, managers must be promoters in order to be effective. Southwest changed the airline business because those in charge thought outside the box and tried something new. Managers must know their limits, but they must also go outside their comfort zone and try to improve their department, which means trying something different while monitoring results.

CASE STUDY 8 ASSESSMENT

1. **What is the main point of Case Study #8?** This case illustrates how decisions may be made at a new company and how some decisions may be made outside of what could be considered the safety zone. There are inherent risks in new ways of thinking but also huge rewards.

2. **Did Southwest utilize a traditional SWOT?** Most likely not from a textbook perspective, but analyze the moves made by Southwest: one Strength was the element of surprise, one Weakness was that Southwest was small and offered limited services compared to other airlines, one Opportunity was to venture into the Internet space before everyone else did, and one Threat was that the desired Internet response would not happen and that the customers would go elsewhere.

3. **Who benefited by Southwest's radical decision?** Southwest, its employees, and its customers

CASE CHALLENGE

Choose another business that seems worthy and do a brief SWOT on it.

34

QUALITY

Productivity and efficiency can be achieved only step by step with sustained hard work, relentless attention to details and insistence on the highest standards of quality and performance. — J. R. D. Tata

CHAPTER PREVIEW

1
Managers cannot overstate the importance of quality.

2
Making high-quality products may equal above average return on investment.

3
Tools now exist to help generate and maintain superior control.

No matter what the business is, it will not flourish unless the quality of the product or service produced remains high. Some argue that quality does not matter in a monopoly market, but it does. Bad quality breeds bad service.

The topic of quality has been well-published in manufacturing as it relates to programs like ISO 9000 and other types of auditing systems, which we will touch on, but the meaning of quality in general must not be taken lightly. Messages about quality must be repeated until every employee gets it.

Managers in every industry must establish where quality standards will be maintained, from restaurants to banking. Service to the customer is obviously imperative, but if the quality of the service and product is lacking, it reflects on both the organization and the management of the organization.

One measurement of management is how quality is maintained. With all of the new auditing programs that have been introduced over the last thirty years, such as ISO 9000, quality is one of the first areas that is audited by outside, independent groups. Again, audits are not limited to manufacturing.

> **One measurement of management is how quality is maintained.**

The finance world consistently audits financial records.[141] Service businesses audit the number of surveys taken by and the comments made by past customers.

Another tool used by service businesses are customer ratings. In manufacturing, businesses receive ratings from their customers, which are then put on file. Some of these ratings are now listed on company websites for all management personnel to see. Based on these tools, a manager may note if his system is working, or if problems are present, he may pinpoint where the problems are so that he may adjust quickly.

A good quality system is like a GPS. A person may know where they want to go but not whether they are going in the right direction. They pull out a GPS to find the correct information, and the GPS tells them how to get where they are going. The same thing is true with a well-documented quality system.

General Electric (GE) provides us with an example of a quality system in which quality was taken seriously. When Jack Welsh was in charge, he mandated that GE use a system called Six Sigma. GE did not develop the syswtem, but it did bring Six Sigma to the forefront in manufacturing circles.

From 2001 to 2003, it was expected that GE would save more than $5 billion due to the benefits of the Six Sigma program, which featured better-defined processes, less time needed for production, and overall improved efficiencies of the operations that were reviewed[18] While it is not evident what the Six Sigma program, which began late in 1995, saved GE, revenue at GE was roughly $26.8 billion the year before Jack Welch became CEO in 1980. Five years after the start of the Six Sigma program, revenue increased to $130 billion.[140]

Other organizations saw how lucrative the Six Sigma program was for GE, so a wave of companies initiated their own programs, such as Dow Chemical, Allied Signal, and Honeywell. Some companies had Six Sigma before GE, but Jack Welsh was more vocal than most about its benefits.[18]

Why is Six Sigma being discussed at this point? It takes complete commitment on the part of management to make quality systems work. This means that all topics covered in previous chapters must be used to motivate all personnel.

What Six Sigma and Lean manufacturing do for quality is to bring the trouble areas to light. Both programs are normally tied together. Six Sigma uses statistics to dig deep into an organization to find the best way to run it. It analyzes why a process requires each action and compares results to the required quality standards. This allows for controls far above what competitors may utilize. Lean manufacturing then looks at why a process, inventory, or movements are performed in a non-efficient or redundant manner and then cleans the whole process up.

Again, this is why management as a whole must buy into the entire program for it to succeed. The end result is a streamlined, smooth, continuous improvement program. Six Sigma and Lean are not just for manufacturing operations. Restaurants and banks have used these methods by following the motions of individuals to see how many times they follow the same path over and over, determining which functions may be streamlined. These tools are used by numerous companies, but this normally begins with managers.[70]

CHAPTER 34
ASSESSMENT

1. **Quality and management go hand-in-hand .Why?** You may have management and some quality, but without competent management you will not have superior quality. Quality must be lived and breathed into the system everyday if employees are to believe in producing products of high quality.

2. **Do quality programs work?** As with any other program, implementing a program and getting people to see the need for it does help, but programs become stale, and quality is no different. Programs work but sometimes need to be modified to keep people interested.

CHAPTER CHALLENGE

Find and write about a quality program that you know of that is being used, and describe why it is working.

35

SUPPLIERS

CHAPTER PREVIEW

1

Do not underestimate a supplier's value.

2

Maintain outstanding communications with suppliers.

3

Do a background check of new and present suppliers.

One area of management that is sometimes overlooked is supplier controls. Suppliers are crucial to a company's ability to function. A supplier must deliver what it has promised. Suppliers are often the weak link in a company's chain. Yes, suppliers are part of their customers' team.

Managers would like to say, *I gave you a purchase order, now supply it, period!* That is how a fool would manage.

Suppliers are critical to maintaining and completing a production flow process, whether in manufacturing or fast food. As members of your team, your suppliers must be motivated. Suppliers must understand that they must deliver quality goods and do it on time.

If a supplier's price is not the lowest, it does not mean that you should not use it. As W. Edwards Deming said, *Do not judge suppliers by price alone.*[32] A manager is responsible for getting suppliers to understand that his organization is the only one that counts. Your management team must maintain a two-way feedback system to assure that suppliers understand that your organization does appreciate their efforts but that the supplier must deliver day-in and day-out.

Certifying bodies such as ISO 9000, TS 16949, and others require absolute control of suppliers, which includes required audits of the suppliers, descriptions on purchase orders sent to the suppliers, annual letters of changes, and improvements. Supplier ratings must be sent to the suppliers to help ensure consistent product, delivery, and communications.[44]

Imagine that you are buying an appliance at a well-known store after putting a lot of research into finding the right model at the right price. You check on the website or

> 66
>
> **Suppliers are often the weak link in a company's chain.**
>
> 99

call the store and are told that a new supply will be coming in tomorrow from the supplier. You give the salesman a down payment to hold the product or buy it outright. The next day, you call the store, to be sure, and are told that the appliance is not there yet. This goes on for a couple of days.

The question then becomes: Is this an internal concern for the company, or is it a supplier problem? The answer is, who cares? The company got the bad reputation, not the supplier. The company may have lost future sales and now has to decide if it wants to continue buying products from this supplier or go elsewhere.

This highlights the key role that the supplier plays in the reputation of an organization and how the supplier/organization communication lines needs to be maintained. Suppliers are an integral part of any company.

Keeping the above information in mind, the basic rules of selecting a supplier comes down to two things, finances and history. The first items for any manager to review include the annual cost of materials from a given supplier, types of cycle inventory control, pipeline inventory, and annual inventory costs, which will equal total annual costs plus freight and administrative costs.[70] These costs are pretty much black and white, and it is easy to compare different suppliers.

History and reputation are not always so black and white, however, and are sometimes trickier to determine. Certifications like ISO 9000 that suppliers may have assist companies in making decisions, but ISO 9000 by itself is not enough. A manager must use other tools.

One tool, the Dun & Bradstreet report, is based on voluntary information offered by most companies.[29] This report is broken into categories, including all owners, any money owed, any lawsuits filed against the company, and length of time that it takes the company to pay its bills. This report, and other similar reports, give the reader a sense of the company.[12]

Using certification information and financial reports, a manager may usually pick a reliable supplier. After the first six to twelvemonths, suppliers should be re-examined to verify that they remain in sound condition. After several audits, some credibility will begin to build. Then, it would be hoped, the company may avoid a scenario like that outlined above.

CHAPTER 35
ASSESSMENT

1. **A business is only as good as its suppliers. Why?** Even though a supplier works for its customers, it may also impact the customer's reputation, so as the customer, you must pick a supplier that will not let you down.

2. **The best way to pick a supplier is price, correct?** The best way to pick a supplier is not price but qualifications, reputation, and a solid financial position. Price should be used as a tiebreaker between two evenly matched suppliers.

CHAPTER CHALLENGE

Find and write about a business where a supplier caused a business to lose its reputation and why.

36

GLOBAL DESTINY

To ensure continuing prosperity in the global economy, nothing is more important than the development and application of knowledge and skills. — Martin Rees

CHAPTER PREVIEW

1
Know the links of your chain.

2
A too long chain is unproductive.

3
A firm chain equals thorough communications.

One fact of life in the past was that most businesses in the United States stayed within the United States, and suppliers were also within the United States. This is not the case any longer. It does not matter what size business you run, bigger business transactions now take place outside the United States.

With China having roughly 20 percent of the world's population, it goes to figure that as China's citizens become acclimated to U.S. products, they will want the products for themselves, so China will be a hot market.

This revolution has already begun with products such as Kentucky Fried Chicken, McDonald's, Smuckers, General Motors, and even Tiffany & Co.[28] China will require products and services from a wide range of countries and businesses, so as a manager, you have a responsibility to review where your business may offer products and/or services outside U.S. borders.

Managing business outside of the United States is not the same as doing business within the United States, and so it requires an adapted approach. The first requirement would be to find an intermediary who knows the country, laws, and the people who are familiar with the country in which you wish to do business. A management team needs to stay on top of the U.S. market but also keep track of the world market and make doing global business part of the business plan.

Inversely, the world market is competing against all markets within the United States, so from both a marketing per-

> **With so much more world-wide competition than ever before, managers must react faster when buying and selling...**

spective and a supplier perspective, a manager must be aware of who is buying similar products and who is selling similar products and adapt quickly.

With so much more worldwide competition than ever before, managers must react faster when buying and selling in order to gain the advantage over similar companies.

After a decision is made to get into the global marketplace, for either buying or selling, it is evident that all previous chapters of this book do come into play. *Global Manifest Destiny*, a book by John A. Caslione and Andrew R. Thomas, lays out a whole plan about how to handle business overseas. The book itself is laid out in global sections to manage:

1. Culture

2. Marketing

3. Account Management

4. Customer Service

5. Procurement

6. Operations

7. Finance

8. Leveraging

9. Other miscellaneous items[24]

Running a business overseas involves practices comparable to those outlined above, but the people and life in the United States are different than in China, and so are the basic business principles. A new manager must follow paths similar to those described in previous chapters of this book, but a special attention is needed to learn about the foreign culture, the language, and money. A new manager needs knowledge and motivation to make it all work.

We are covering this subject now, as there is no way that any business in the United States will be able to avoid doing business overseas at some time in the near future, so now is the time to learn.

CHAPTER 36
ASSESSMENT

1. **Small-to medium-sized businesses in the United States should not have to worry about buying or selling overseas, right?** Wrong. Most new customers are not in the U.S. but in foreign countries like China, so all businesses in the United States must be aware of the possibilities that foreign countries offer.

2. **Nine items that a new person/business should be aware of when dealing with companies overseas are?** Culture, Marketing, Account Management, Customer Service, Procurement, Operations, Finance, Leveraging, Other miscellaneous items

3. **These nine items sound easy, but why are they not?** Ways of life and languages are different in a foreign country, so it takes time for a new manager to learn about other countries.

CHAPTER CHALLENGE

Find and write about a company that is mainly in the U.S. that could benefit from foreign exposure, and describe how this could be done.

PART V

WRAPPING IT UP

37

LOOPING IT ALL TOGETHER

In this age, which believes that there is a short cut to everything, the greatest lesson to be learned is that the most difficult way is, in the long run, the easiest. — Henry Miller

CHAPTER PREVIEW

1 Never stop looking at yourself.

2 The suggestions made in this book work.

3 Every lesson has value.

As life itself teaches us, we are never finished learning, but we must keep our mind open to understand this message. In my case, I learned after years of working hard that I needed to loop all of my knowledge together, but something was missing — a college degree. I had sound fundamentals, but my overall knowledge-base was still lacking, so with a dedicated wife and three young children, I decided to reach for all of the knowledge necessary to do my job better, but also to understand that the more information and know-how I had under my belt, the better I could make decisions with favorable outcomes.

It took me thirteen years to complete my first degree, but it was well worth the time. As we have learned in this book, education and knowledge are stepping-stones to success. Learning does not have to be quantified by a college degree because any outside education will help to broaden the scope of awareness.

The first lesson I learned was as beneficial as the latest lesson learned. I have not stop learning, nor should a manager ever stop learning, because what is learned accumulates and becomes wisdom, which brings us full circle.

As an accumulation of all points discussed in previous chapters, Case Study #9 takes into account what an executive-level management group must decide in terms of the future of an organization. This last Case Study illustrates all points that management must think about when making critical decisions, but it also shows the complexity of the investigations prior to making a final decision and how executives had to investigate and then decide what the facts were.

> **As life itself teaches us, we are never finished learning.**

Even though some management decisions appear easy, a lot of work must be done to make decisions that many people would not consider or make correctly. Case Study #9 illuminates the work that must go into a well thought-out decision. It also evidences a culmination of practices that executives must utilize to have the best chance of achieving their goals.

This information, if used correctly, will prevent failures, from day-to-day activities to long-term planning.

CHAPTER 37
ASSESSMENT

1. **Why is it best to keep an open mind?** A person with an open mind may realize that self-improvement may take place anywhere and at anytime.

2. **How may the topics in this book be used?** Case Study #9 will illustrate where the topics discussed here come up in real-life business situations and how having knowledge about these topics may help in making better decisions.

CHAPTER CHALLENGE

Find and write about a person from any time period who recognized that it was still not too late to learn.

CASE STUDY 9

A COMPANY'S LIFE

CASE GOALS

1	**2**	**3**
Demonstrate how ideas from this book are used in the real world of business.	Management decisions require a lot of review to make things work.	Realize that some decisions are difficult.

In a previous chapter, we discussed SWOT and how it could be used for middle-management decision-making options, but in this chapter we will discuss SWOT for executive-level management. At this level, managers need to decide upon company direction, public stocks offerings versus remaining a private entity, investments, as well as other critical decisions to lead the company's survival.

These decisions deal with money, jobs, and people's livelihoods. In this Case Study, a decision must be made whether to keep a company private, or allow it to be purchased by a more dominant organization, or merge it with another company. The facts of this case are real, and decisions surrounding this case have been discussed numerous times. Every case is personal, and managers have a responsibility to the organization but also to the employees.

The Case Study below is from an actual college thesis, but it has been condensed for our purposes here. However, key points remain to show how far management must think into the future to protect a company and to keep day-to-day operations running smoothly. Again, this Case Study may be used in any type of business. Each kind of business will have its own points of interest, but the decisions will be similar in nature.

The below Case Study show cases many areas of management knowledge, including SWOT, so that managers may learn how to make the best possible decisions. Text in parentheses in this Case Study refers to the chapter title in which the subject matter was previously covered in the book.

The genesis of this Case Study is an 80-year-old business for which the owner has a decision to make: employee buyout, leveraged buyout or merger. Meaning sell to the employees and continue business as usual, or sell outright and not know the plans of the future buyer, or find another business that can benefit or compliment by combining the two businesses together. The company is real but must remain anonymous in this text for purposes of privacy. For this reason, we will call this company the XYZ Company.

Managers of XYZ had to determine which of the three choices, employee buyout, leverage buyout or merger, would be best for the owner, the employees, and the community. The second-generation owner was in his eighties and had no heirs to take over the business (Strategic Planning).

Executives made a decision to look at all options in order to keep the business running profitably in the future.

On a fundamental level, this scenario may be likened to having an older car, so you buy a new car. You buy a new car, you and your partner share the old and new car and use both economically (merger), sell the old car to your child but still insure it (employee buyout), or scrap it so that you have a clean break (leveraged buyout). It would be nice if all business transactions were this easy, but they are not.

The XYZ Company operated in the metal contract manufacturing business. Its main business function was to make steel component parts for bigger companies. The component parts went into transmissions in marine, aerospace, and mining vehicles, as well as forklifts.

The market had been devastated by economic downfalls, with a number of businesses failing and going into bankruptcy, so determining the proper direction for XYZ's future was difficult (Unknown External Factors). This limited some options for mergers because of a declining competition base. However, XYZ had promoted a continuous improvement philosophy throughout its years in business that emphasized the business's value.[121]

As stated above, the number of competitors had shrunk, however, a reasonable number of companies could still be considered for a merger, found in different locations and in a variety of sizes. Competitor sales ranged from $50 million to $23.5 billion annually in 2011.

To compound the problem, in a good way, a variety of other businesses were interested in what XYZ had been able to accomplish.[121] It had multiple capabilities allowing it to compete in an assortment of product-fulfilling arenas (Innovation).

Because of customers in common, different companies were aware of this organization. Moreover, XYZ had pushed into additional markets to continue diversifying its product base. This range of capabilities made a merger appear to be the best option. Because competition still existed, an abundance of options for mergers and employee or leveraged buyouts was recognized.

The list of manufacturing businesses within each of the three buyout choices above required that planning be done well in advance of the final decision, meaning that attention had to be given to all options immediately.

A list was made to denote the pros and cons of a merger, an employee buyout, and a leveraged buyout so that a final conclusion could be drawn while keeping the present owner's interests, the employees, and the community in mind.

A merger was considered first as the best option, as cash was not as much of a factor as it was with the buyout options. However, other conditions needed to be overcome if a merger was to work. A detailed report describing what constituted a merger and how that affected the company was put together.

First, was a merger the best choice for XYZ? Questions and concerns had to be analyzed before moving forward. As of 2008, mergers in general had increased over past historical numbers. But a percentage of these companies that jumped on the merger bandwagon merged too quickly, without doing thorough research about the dangers and pitfalls that existed when two companies combined their business and financial records and practices[14] (Investigate Solutions).

A merger would be an excellent strategic move (Strategic Planning), but both companies involved had to look far into the future to decide in what direction the merger would take them.[14] Details that needed to be reviewed included the business entities themselves, legal agreements, branding, who owned what, and where the combining of the companies would fall in the marketplace.[14]

Goals for both XYZ and another company would be to make a lucrative deal (Goals for the Future). The advantage for a small business was the possibility that a merger would help to expand its business more rapidly.[14]

As stated by Martin Harshberger, who specializes in strategic planning and pre- and post-merger integration, "A merger of two companies was very much like any other partnership, just larger and more complex."

Mergers don't always work out the way they've been planned (Conflict Happens). All management personnel do not always have the shareholders' interests at stake, but rather their own. The interest in the business is not for the merger to succeed, but what may certain individuals get out of the business.

While reviewing the possible merger option, the group putting the merger plan together had to make sure the shareholders' interests were protected (People: The Right Choice). Some of the concerns that would had to be examined more closely were:

1. **Manager's hubris:** This is a manager's over-confidence about expectations, which sometimes results in one company paying more for another company than its true value. In the case of a merger, the manager of company A knows that company B is worth X number of dollars, but the manager thinks he can get 10 percent more out of the deal, so he pays more for company B than it is worth. This includes investments, personnel, or improvements that do not develop after money is invested.

2. **Empire-building:** Managers want large companies to manage, thereby building their own power.

3. **Managers' compensation:** Certain executive management groups are paid based on total profits of a company instead of per ratio or share, so managers have a special interest in increasing total profits.[68]

Consideration had to be given to opinions and feelings of personnel within each organization, as emotions could run high with both employees and shareholders. When employees do not know what is going to happen, personal concerns escalate. When the news of a merger is announced to employees, their concerns are about their futures and this becomes their number one worry (Honesty).

This type of emotion affected quality, production, and deliveries at a time when XYZ needed to maintain high levels of each. At this point, it would have been difficult for the company to over-communicate (Respect Is Necessary).[71]

A lot of effort had to be put into maintaining employees' importance to XYZ and to the merger (Figure 15).

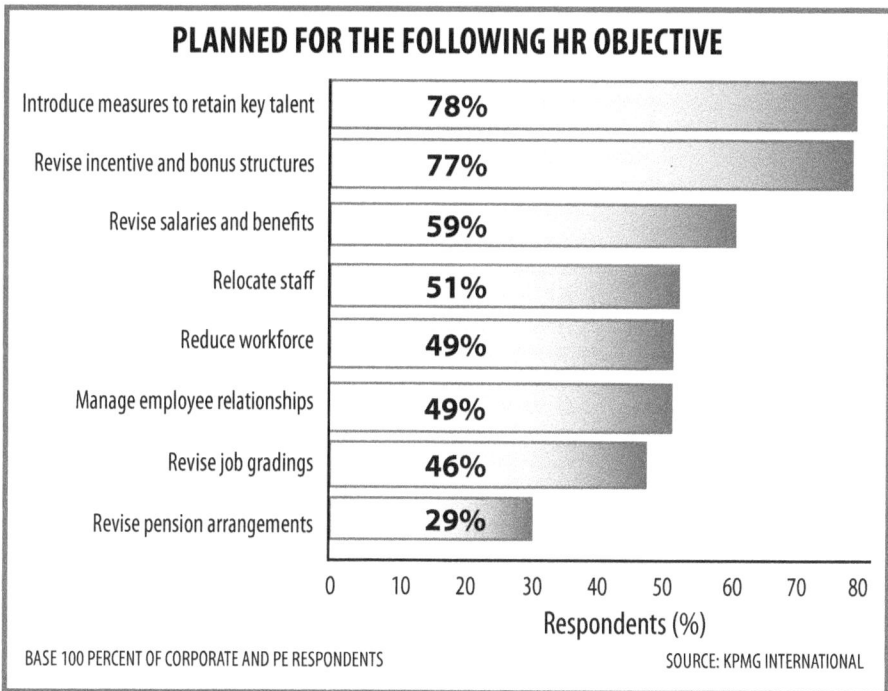

PLANNED FOR THE FOLLOWING HR OBJECTIVE

HR Objective	Respondents (%)
Introduce measures to retain key talent	78%
Revise incentive and bonus structures	77%
Revise salaries and benefits	59%
Relocate staff	51%
Reduce workforce	49%
Manage employee relationships	49%
Revise job gradings	46%
Revise pension arrangements	29%

BASE 100 PERCENT OF CORPORATE AND PE RESPONDENTS

SOURCE: KPMG INTERNATIONAL

FIGURE 15: HUMAN RESOURCES OBJECTIVES FOR A MERGER.[65]

The goal of a merger was to build confidence for a long-term, beneficial relationship for both companies. High numbers of mergers fail because the people in charge look more closely at short-term factors.

This concept was not new. A phenomenon known as The Great Merger Movement of the 1890s, during which companies merged to reduce production costs in a hurry, but caused higher sales prices to the end customer of the company's product, due to the actual costs/effects of merging.[72]

It was easy for those involved to see day-to-day operations of each organization because of visits and meetings with employees, but long-term goals and business planning were taken more seriously when decisions needed to be made and options were being considered. The short-term is easy to see, but to make a merger last, serious thought should be given to the merger in order to predict the direction that both businesses will travel.

Government laws and Acts have been put into place to curtail what had been seen as a lack of long-term planning and short-term greed at the costs of communities and employee jobs.[96] Some of the controls put into place to monitor mergers include (The Law And Management):

1. The Sherman Act: to control mergers that may create a monopoly.

2. The Clayton Act: to control where mergers lessen competition or allow for discrimination.

3. The Hart-Scott-Rodino Act: requires pre-merger notification to the government antitrust agencies to check for the likely effects of a merger before it takes place.

The Federal Trade Commission has implemented various other laws and Acts.[129] However, some mergers from the 1990s and 2000s are viewed as successful:

1. Exxon and Mobil, 1998

2. Bell Atlantic and GTE, 2000

3. Pfizer and Warner–Lambert, 2000

4. AOL and Time Warner, 1999 to 2002 (this merger ultimately failed)

5. Procter & Gamble and Gillette, 2005

6. Pfizer and Wyeth, 2009[12]

When the buyout option was examined, the owner had two choices, an employee buyout or a leveraged buyout. The employee buyout (EBO) was considered first on behalf of the employees, followed by the shareholders, ownership, and lastly financial considerations. An EBO is a re-structuring strategy wherein the employees buy the majority of the stake in the company. The EBO was viewed as an attractive alternative to a leveraged buyout.[61]

The pre-existing condition of XYZ was critical. Either the company was sitting well financially or it was financially distressed, which would have made for alarming conditions under which employees would want to buy the company. In contemplating an EBO, executives needed to make sure that XYZ did not spiral into a financially distressed condition (Economics: The Root Of All Evil).[61]

The usual steps taken in an EBO are that the company's assets are sold to the employees through an employee stock option, so that a minimum of 51 percent of the company is then owned by the employees.[61]

Ownership would be shared for a variety of reasons, and they hoped an employee buyout would be viewed as the right thing to do. However, even though it was viewed as the right thing for employees, it was also thought to be the most practical method of keeping the business going as usual.[94]

An EBO did have benefits for both the new owners (the employees) and XYZ (Job Satisfaction). Some of these benefits were:

1. The move would help attract and retain the best employees. Small businesses have a difficult time finding above-average employees, so employee ownership is an enticement.

2. Buying out an owner who has no more interest in the business.

3. An EBO was a method by which the present owner could raise capital, so that he could use that capital to invest in a totally different project or business, if he desired.

4. Business performance tends to improve when employees own the company.

5. EBOs give tax benefits to all employees for certain ownership structures.[94]

6. There would be lower workers compensation costs and/or health-care costs with higher long-term ownership value.[19,93]

Even though an EBO sounded like the best choice, there were some down sides as well:

1. The different personalities of the many employees involved were problematic.

2. More legal contract language needed to be stated up front.[94]

    a. Wrongful acts.

    b. Partnership liabilities.

    c. Who would be the decision maker, how to terminate the EBO if all goes wrong.

    d. The type of partnership (limited liability corporation, S-corporation, or C-corporation).

All of the above would make the legal part of the process a challenge.[94] Knowing all of this meant that executives had to review and possibly re-define the business (Company Culture).

In addition to legal matters, there were tax concerns. How the company structured the EBO could result in either the company or the employees paying more taxes.[94]

Employees would have to pay a certain amount in taxes for the types of shares of stock that they would receive from the company as part of the EBO arrangement only when they quit or retired. The company would deduct from the taxes that it paid the number of shares given to employees. If employees received shares as a gift, they could choose to pay taxes at a gift tax value, but taxes would still have to be paid.

All of these points had to be reviewed with legal counsel prior to any agreement to avoid costing XYZ or the employees more money.[94]

Most importantly, all of the above points were thought about well before the possible cultural change. Employees had to determine if they were interested, and the original owner had to determine what method of transfer of ownership would assure the best outcome and guarantee payment to himself.[23]

The owner would need to inform all employees involved of the details in advance: whether employees would accept the buyout, financing, legal terms, who and how the new management was going to direct, and the present ownership agreements. This would have to be accomplished through a series of company-wide show-and-tell meetings with all employees, which required lots of time (Presentations).[23] The first tool used to determine whether an EBO was a viable option was a survey given to all personnel who would be involved in the EBO. The results of the survey were published to all employees, then the decision was made whether to go forward based upon the results of the survey (Documentation, Audits: A Manager's Eyes).[23]

Finally, the simplest form of a buyout would have been a leveraged buyout (LBO). The most relevant factor here was financing. With a leveraged buyout, a new owner had the ability to borrow up to 90 percent of the purchase price of the company.[42] This practice was common in the 1980s with bigger companies, but most failed due to the quality of debt used. Which means that the company taking over borrowed money in a risky fashion, so if the business did not make a lot of cash in a hurry, the loans went unpaid.[42]

For small businesses, the most common LBOs were done by management personnel within the company being sold, by purchasing pieces or shares of the company or receiving benefits in place of wage increases or bonuses.[42]

The downside of an LBO in this case was that the new ownership could face some precarious considerations, which involved a weak market position, high finance charges, a feeble customer base, and high operations costs, because of the poor economy at that time.[42] If an LBO was determined to be the correct option, it had to be acted on far in advance to avoid or at least think about the issues listed above. A plan to avoid difficult markets with customers or the economy as a whole would need to be developed. This is why management would need more time to work out the far-reaching set of plans.[42]

The advantage of the LBO was that executives could make a commitment that current management would remain in place for a given time period. This would be accomplished with meetings with both parties involved in the

LBO, in which executives are normally part of the negotiation group for the company being sold. Customers would not be concerned then and take their business elsewhere, and an increased effort to improve financial incentives for others in management enabled improved productivity and loyalty.[42]

Because of so much past publicity, LBOs were not viewed in high regard by most people, so explaining the actual details broken down clearly and precisely to the present owner was very important (Performance Is Key). The new owners may focus on certain points that they like, but may miss other critical items that would not be seen until later. However, the current owner would have his cash, and all ties would be completely severed for a clean break.[42] The company, with all of its older employees, might then fail, leaving good workers out of a job.

The most difficult area to control and maintain throughout the change in ownership would be personnel. To sustain an organization requires a lot of effort and foresight from previous and new management groups, which becomes a two-step process that necessitates a lot of communication[71] (Organizational Structure).

(Figure 16) illustrates the value of human capital compared to social capital, which is the value that employees provide to an organization. With the change of ownership, all of these factors would be crucial for a smooth transition.[71]

Kurt Lewin, a social psychologist, received accolades for his theories about organizational change. Highlights of Lewin's Change Model include learning something new, clear motivation, people are the central point, resistance to change is inevitable, and consistent reinforcement is needed.[71]

When the company's owner decided that a change in ownership was needed, a transition group had to realize that certain personnel traits would play into how the ownership change would affect all employees, so Lewin's change model was reviewed to understand and prevent confusion in how to handle any changes that would take place.

It is worth noting that together with Lewin's model, XYZ also used the Eight Steps to Leading Organizational Change, conceived by John Kotter, an expert in leadership and change management. Features of Kotter's Eight Steps include establish a sense of urgency, create the guiding coalition, develop a vision, communicate, eliminate barriers, generate short-term

STRATEGIC BELIEFS:
People, individually and
collectively are the key to
an organization's success.

INDIVIDUAL HUMAN CAPITAL	SOCIAL CAPITAL
1. Intelligence/abilities/knowledge	1. Shared visions/goals
2. Visions/dreams/aspirations	2. Shared values
3. Technical and social skills	3. Trust
4. Confidence/self-esteem	4. Mutual respect/good will
5. Initiative/entrepreneurship	5. Friendship/support groups
6. Adaptability/flexibility	6. Mentoring/positive role modeling
7. Readiness to learn	7. Participation/empowerment
8. Creativity	8. Connections/sources
9. Enthusiasm	9. Networks/affiliations
10. Motivation/commitment	10. Cooperation/collaboration
11. Persistence	11. Teamwork
12. Ethical standards/courage	12. Camaraderie
13. Honesty	13. Assertive, non-aggressive communication
14. Emotional maturity	14. Functional conflict
	15. Win-win negotiations/philanthropy/volunteering

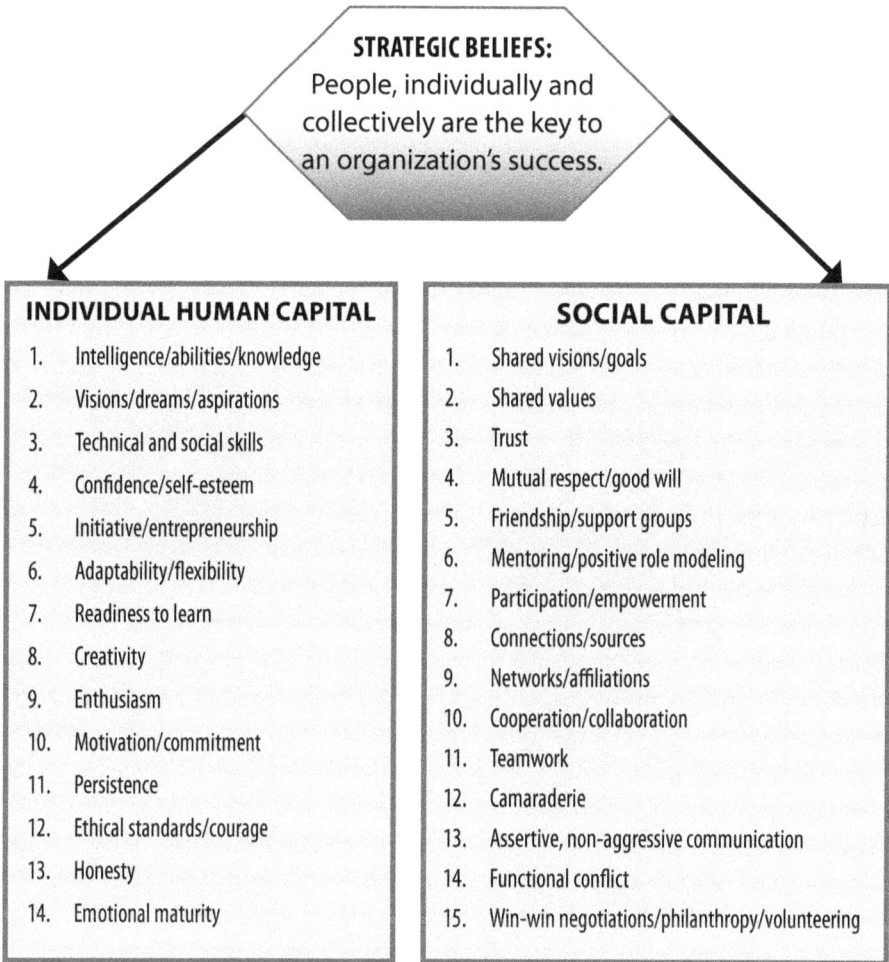

FIGURE 16: ORGANIZATIONAL BEHAVIOR.
KREITNER, R. (2010).NEW YORK: MCGRAW-HILL.

wins, produce more change, anchor new approaches[71] (Implement Action With Objectives).

With the use of the above-mentioned key elements, the transition in ownership may be accomplished a lot smoother with a far better chance of long-term success, success being a result of motivation (Motivation).[71]

After all three options were researched, the information had to be compared to XYZ's SWOT to determine which choice made the most sense.[121] The points used for comparison were:

1. **Strengths:** zero debt, engineering knowledge.

2. **Weaknesses:** ownership succession, heavy dependence on a limited number of customers.

3. **Opportunities:** excellent quality and delivery reputation for additional work with new customers; obtaining new quality certifications in areas of ISO 9000, TS 16949, and NADCAP aerospace.

4. **Threats:** competition from similar-sized companies to large corporations and uncertain succession plans for executives.[121]

Decision-makers found that between the three options, merger, EBO, or LBO, the decision was not easy. All options had pros and cons. The germane point to consider was that both previous and new owners should have planned far in advance of any change in ownership.

Availability of funds would not be a factor, as numerous choices existed, such as employee stock options, up to 90 percent of XYZ's value in loans, investment groups, and government loans. Because there is a value with the present company and many more people are now owners, there could be opportunities for new businesses through contacts with other companies both financially and product wise that could be part of a future merger or leveraged buyout.[12,122] However, communication to all employees was lacking, no matter what option for new ownership was selected.

A leveraged buyout was not viewed as the best option. However, it was the cleanest method for the present owner to break off all ties with XYZ. As for the future viability of the company, a leveraged buyout was the most difficult in terms of employee relations, transitions, and goals for XYZ to receive the required return on investment, all leading to overall higher risks.

Research on all options helped executives determine that a merger was the best choice. The SWOT test confirmed this.

After all information pointed to a merger as the best choice, the next step was using D.R. King's eleven rules for a successful merger. A list of pros and cons was constructed for each point using the SWOT to better detail why there were pros or cons:

1. Gaining market share was possible because of the top four customers that XYZ already had, which was a strength that made it attractive to other organizations.

2. Economies of scale, in particular declining or stagnant markets that were present due to U.S. economic conditions, sales, and the lackluster business climate that had existed were compared to XYZ's market, which was also weak in most areas but strong in the transmission component markets. XYZ's business was going well in one market but needed to improve in others, so the correct fit would be an opportunity for both companies.

3. Enabling access to products or services is a viable way to keep or improve a dying business. One area that XYZ wanted to break into was the medical field, but so far it had been unable to do this. With the right merger, getting into the medical field was possible, but XYZ's weakness was that its offerings had limitations.

4. Expanding geographically was a positive choice after the market peaked. The Midwest region was the primary territory for XYZ, so the eastern and western United States held possibilities for expansion. At the time of the merger, though, its limited number of locations were seen as a weakness.

5. Both companies combining their best assets would facilitate faster growth than would be possible for each individual company. XYZ had satisfactory equipment and zero debt but did not possess knowledge of all processes necessary for handling steel products, so other steel processes could have complemented theirs. This would be an opportunity for both organizations.[54]

6. Economy of scope to be considered in marketing, and distribution of different types of products became critical in order to reduce traffic costs while expanding exposure. XYZ's marketing and distribution were limited, which opened up more possibilities for a merger, but at the time of the analysis, it was a weakness because of a lack of marketing and traffic skills.

7. Although increased opportunities of managerial specialization or increased order sizes when combining businesses were possible with the correct merger, this was not initially seen. Different management styles and efficiencies would have facilitated a more potent organization.

   XYZ was not heavy in management but was strong in engineering processing that would help other organizations. These limited processes, though, could have led to a threat.

8. Resource transfer could balance out distribution across the firm, so targeting the right company was crucial. This made possible a local-company merger, but it was more likely that a merger would have to be with a company from out of state. An out-of-state choice would have been considered an opportunity.

9. Vertical integration (management positions from supervisor to president go straight up the chain) aids personnel in understanding how the overall management program works and will also help determine if a certain merger will work based on similar management programs. One company's strength could be what the other company is looking for, such as accounting services or, in XYZ's case, engineering knowledge. This would have helped both organizations but had to be considered as both an opportunity and a threat.

10. Acquiring skills instead of hiring would be another reason for the merger. The company offered engineering, production, and sound management services that would combine well with other companies that had stronger marketing and sales departments. This would have led to improved opportunities.

11. Forming one management team from two organizations was a limited concern, but after review of an already reduced management staff, it was realized that it would be an easier task than originally thought. However, even with a smaller combined staff, if everyone did not get along, there would be trouble for both organizations, so it was a concern and a threat.[68]

Based on the above eleven points and the company's SWOT, it was apparent that numerous opportunities would enable XYZ to stay in business (Strategic Planning).[67,121] After the owner reviewed the SWOT, he looked for an organization that offered:

1. A similar market or complimentary products;

2. Wider geographical location;

3. Opportunity for a whole new product type that could be developed with others outside the present organization

4. No financial trouble;

5. Better distribution; and

6. After review, there were additional opinions of different management types and services seen that could be tried

After evaluation, an EBO would not have helped in the areas where the SWOT showed that improvement was necessary, so the likelihood of an EBO was reduced. At the same time, an LBO was still in the running because depending on who the buyout group was, that group would have had to show benefits that were listed as needs in the company's SWOT analysis.

The final step in the evaluation process was a meeting between the company's VPs to discuss all factors that had already been researched by the president of the company.

The outcome of the meeting would determine, both from a management perspective and in terms of financial position, what the executives felt was best to be done with the company. During the meeting, certain key points were explained or clarified:

1. A leveraged buyout was the cleanest and shortest option.

2. If management did not want to wait to make a decision, then time would not allow for longer-term options to be considered.

3. The Annual Business Plan allowed for future options. At the time, the president had decided that an EBO was no longer an option because of the capital that the employees would need to borrow as part of the EBO takeover. The EBO itself becomes a trust fund with

the employees as members. The trust fund borrows the money to pay the owner. The profits pay the loan back, and the employees retain the value of the company. The trust fund value increases when the number of shares increases, and when more profits are made. All are based on the percentage of ownership, which increases as the employees own more of the company.

4. A merger was possible, but time was running out. Finding the right company to merge with and set up a plan would take years to complete.

5. The company's strengths were that it had zero debt, fine relationships with customers, and long-term employees.

6. Finally, the owner of XYZ would select an upper management group to build a plan. This group would have to analyze all options including the owner, the employees, and what outside group is trying to take ownership in order to establish the best chance of success.

When all information was collected from this meeting, it would be apparent that the upper management group would have to determine the direction of a leveraged buyout of some kind, but the group would also have additional options that were detected in the investigation that could have an immediate impact on XYZ's position.

The employees would have loved to buy the company, but due to a lack of money and time, an EBO would have been doomed to fail. Start-up company data, listed in *Small Biz Trends* magazine, showed that failure rates in the first two years of new businesses (and this would have been considered a new business because the responsibility of management and employees alike would change, in addition to financial burdens having increased) were between 64 percent and 75 percent in 2008,and this was true as well through 2012.[111] With the need to borrow such an exorbitant amount of cash, the failure risk would have escalated even more, so an EBO was deemed a high risk.

All of the research suggested that a merger or a leveraged buyout were the remaining options. From the present owner's perspective, it was difficult to accept that a merger was best because he wanted a clean break from the company. A merger was still possible, but the time in which to act was critical. All things considered, a merger was the proper choice, but immediate action was required.

A final determination was hard to make because depending on the vantage point from which all facts we reviewed, the correct decision seemed different. The present owner wanted the business to continue in the same manner that it had for the past eighty years, and with the same namesake, but that was not possible. Staying in business as long as it had was difficult enough, but the required changes in management increased the risk of failure (Organizational Structure).

To recap, a merger scored highest on the thesis author's research table. An EBO would have been the choice of most employees, however, funding an EBO would have been difficult,

> Executives' decisions are complex, which is why a manager needs all of the information in this book. It will enable him to make calculated decisions with better-than-average odds of success.

and the risk of failure was too high to overlook. The ultimate decision made was a leveraged buyout, which was the direction that the present owner felt he needed to go, but this was not the best choice according to the thesis author.

XYZ's future was still in the hands of present management, so with the right merger, benefits such as gain in market share, growth potential, improved branding, better geographic exposure, and expanded skill sets of employees, all added up to keeping the company in the black for a long time. But time and the current owner hindered this option from becoming a reality.

After all research was concluded and evaluated, the thesis author's final decision was that it made the most sense for XYZ to merge with another company, to enhance its business opportunities, then establish a long-term goal to allow a employee buyout option of both organizations combined (Evolution).

As may be seen, some executive decisions are neither simple nor easy to make, and a lot of investigation and knowledge must go into the final decision (Knowledge). Executives' decisions are complex, which is why a manager needs to learn all of the information in this book. It will enable him to make calculated decisions with better-than-average odds of success (Investigate Solutions).

When managers get to a point where they may make decisions like the ones in this Case Study, they have made it to the top and have earned their stripes. But remember, things change over time, and a manager's knowledge must change and expand as well. If one thing needs to remain in the back of a manager's mind, it is to never stop learning, watching, and consistently evolving by paying attention, listening, and most importantly, respecting others.

CASE STUDY 9
ASSESSMENT

1. **What is the purpose of this Case Study?** To illustrate all facets of business managers must understand. Also to illuminate where the information in this book could be used in making decisions.

2. **Are some chapter elements more essential than others?** Depending upon where your management experience is at this point in your career. Knowledge is like steps on a ladder — you may be able to skip one and survive, but miss more than one, and you might crash and burn.

3. **Why were Honesty, Presentations, and Company Culture key chapters used for illustrative purposes in this Case Study?** Honesty shows the character and reliability managers look for. Managers must know how to create and give Presentations, whether speaking to one person or a group. Lastly, Executive-level managers need to know how to set up an organization for continued success, and Company Culture is critical for that.

4. **Even though not all chapters were cited in Case Study 9, was some information from all chapters covered?** Yes. For example, a manager must gain knowledge to effectively plan strategy, and problem-solving skills are a necessity if a manager is to tackle a project like the one featured in this Case Study. Opportunities and problems will always arise that need a manager's attention.

CASE CHALLENGE

Find your own case study and describe how you would use at least two Chapters from each Part (I through IV) of this book.

FINAL COMMENTS

We have explored one central theme in this book. Are managers born, or are they made from what they experience in life? As you may have surmised, I have concluded that the ability to manage comes from life's experiences. Managers need many different tools, but life's experiences provide one with the foundation upon which all other building blocks rest. Some of these experiences are profound, while others are subtle.

Learning to deal with people is a rewarding challenge. Remember, an investment is needed, and, as the old saying goes, the more you put into it, the more you get out of it.

The quest for knowledge is a never-ending one. A manager must be willing to continue to learn. Change is one thing that cannot be stopped, so people's attitudes, tools like electronics and methods of production, and money itself are always changing, and managers must stay on top of these changes. Gaining more knowledge will help a manager become more valuable to an organization, as well as become a more complete manager and person.

Wisdom comes with experience, knowledge, and motivation. A manager might not always make the correct choices as often as she wants to, but she learns by her successes and failures, perhaps most by her failures. Even though you may want to avoid them, embrace failures as the truest learning experiences.

An old supervisor once asked me, "If a manager teaches just six people what he knows, and those six teach six others, what do you think the true effect of one manager can be?"

The effects are endless.

At a certain point, a manager becomes a teacher. It is then that a manager experiences the rewards of his efforts. But even as a teacher, he never stops being a student.

REFERENCES

1. Allison Supplier Quality. (2006). http://www.allisontransmission.com/search-results?indexCatalo gue=all&searchQuery=QSB&wordsMode=.

2. Allison Transmission (2014). http://www.allisontransmission.com/docs/default-source/purchas-ing-forms/qsb-module-3.pdf?sfvrsn=2.

3. Arituso, D. (September 16, 2005). *Southwest Airlines' Anne Murray*. Retrieved August 7, 2010, from IMEDIA connection: http://www.imediaconnection.com/content/6749.imc.

4. Armour, S. R. (May 19, 2011). *Boeing case may prompt change: Firms might have to tell unions of moving plans*. Retrieved June 11, 2011, from Bloomberg News: http://www.postandcourier.com/article/20110519/PC04/305199873.

5. ASCOT & IRWG. (2013). Don't Risk It. RTO/Tourism Crisis Management Group. Retrieved December 2, 2013, from Don't Risk it: www.ret.gov.au/tourism/Documents/business/Resilience-Kit-for.

6. ASQ. (2004). Fishbone (Ishikawa) Diagram Excerpted from Nancy R. Tague's *The Quality Toolbox*. http://asq.org/learn-about-quality/cause-analysis-tools/overview/fishbone.html.

7. Barbee, P. (January 2010). *Walmart Vs. CVS/Pharmacy*. Retrieved June 30, 2011, from Indeed one search, all jobs: http://www.indeed.com/forum/job/pharmacy-technician/Walmart-VS-CVS-Pharmacy/t205404.

8. Benna, D. (September 21, 2009). Key Account Manager General Mills Retail. (A. Jantz Interview).

9. Biller-Safran, F. (September 17, 2010). *America: Melting Pot Of Race And Culture, Or A Loss Of Ethnic Identity*. Retrieved June 15, 2011, from Rise Up : http://www.usaonrace.com/feature-stories/1660/america-a-melting-pot-of-race-and-culture-or-a-loss-of-ethnic-identity.

10. Blanchard, Ken. (2008). *Why is Situational Leadership Important*. Leadership Excellence Journal (May 2008).

11. Blanchard, Ken. (2013). Ken Blanchard-Situational Leadership. Retrieved September 16, 2013, from mftrou.com: http://mftrou.com/ken-blanchard.html.

12. Block, B. Stanley, Geoffrey A. Hirt, Bartley R. Danielson. (2011). *Foundations of Financial Management*. New York, New York: McGraw-Hill Irwin.

13. BossEye, Inc. (2006). *ABC Method of Time Management*. Retrieved April 14, 2013, from TimeAnalyzer: http://timeanalyzer.com/lib/abc.htm.

14. Braith, C. (February 7, 2008). *Pros and cons of merging your small business.* Retrieved November4, 2011, from InsideBusiness: http://www.insidebusiness360.com/index.php/pros-and-cons-of -merging-your- small-business-27337/.

18. Brassard, Michael. Diane Ritter. (2001). *Sailing Through Six Sigma.* Capital Offset Company, Inc., Concord, NH.

19. Brown, G. (August 2009). *Workers Compensation Return-to-Work Programs: Cost Savers?* Retrieved December 10, 2011, from IRMI.com: http://www.irmi.com/expert/articles/2009/armc08-insurance-claims-management.aspx.

20. Brush, Michael. (2011). How Target is gaining on Wal-Mart. Retrieved December 15, 2013, from MSN Money: http://money.msn.com/how-to-invest/how-target-is-gaining-on-wal-mart-brush.aspx.

21. Bureau, I. A. (2002). *Quality system assessment checklist.* Detroit. MI: ANFIA.

22. Business Management Systems. (2012). 2-2 3-2 2-3 Rotating Shift Schedule. Retrieved December 14, 2013, from Business Management System: http://community.bmscentral.com/learnss/ZC/c4tr12-4.

23. Businesslink. (2011). *Why consider an employee buyout?* Retrieved November 12, 2011, from Business Link: http://www.businesslink.gov.uk/bdotg/action/detail?itemId=1077627473&type=RESOURCES.

24. Caslione, John A., Andrew R. Thomas. (2002). *Global Manifest Destiny.* Chicago, Illinois: Dearborn Trade Publishing.

25. CAW. (June 22, 2011). *First Group of Magna Workers Join CAW Under the Framework of Fairness.* Retrieved February 22, 2011, from Auto Spector: http://www.autospectator.com/cars/union-activity/0033815-first-group-magna-workers-join-caw-under-framework-fairness.

26. Churchill, R. (April 2, 2001). *Southwest Airlines Power a sales liftoff.* Retrieved August 7, 2010, from Brandweek: http://findarticles.com/p/articles/mi_m0BDW/is_14_42/ai_72981547.

27. Clough, V. (May 1, 2000). Personal Motivation vs. Prior Knowledge Levels: Assessing the Impact of Internal Conditions upon Training Outcomes for Adult Learners of Technology in a Federal Workplace. Retrieved June 24, 2011, from Georgetown University: http://cct.georgetown.edu/65301.html.

28. Cho, H. Janet. (2013). China wants more U.S.-made products, government says. Retrieved March 8, 2014, from http://www.cleveland.com/business/index.ssf/2013/01/china_wants_more_us-made_produ.html.

29. D&B. (2013). Welcome to D&B, where critical business decisions can be made with confidence. Retrieved December 15,2013, from D&B About Us: http://www.dnb.com/company.html.

30. KPMG, I. (2008). All to play for Striving for post deal success. United Kingdom: KPMG. Lemons, D., M. O'Kane, & A. Wurth (2005). *Next Generation Human Resources: Driving Organizational Excellence*. Houston, Texas: APQC.

31. Deming, W. E. (1975). *On Statistical Aids Toward Economic Production*. The Institute of Management Science, Interface Vol. 5, No. 4, Aug 1975.

32. Deming, W. E. (1988). *Out of Crisis*. Cambridge, Mass: MIT.

33. Deveau, S. (May 4, 2011). *Stronach's parting words: Avoid debt*. Retrieved June 22, 2011, from Financial Post: http://business.financialpost/2011/05/04/stronachs-parting-word-avoid-debt.

34. Eckert, A. (August 1, 2009). 09/10 Southwest Airlines Co-op. *California find yourself here*. Los Angles, California, USA: Visit California.

35. ECS. (2013). Case History From XYZ. Racine, WI.

36. Edgar Online. (July 16, 2002). *Magna International Inc*. Retrieved May 6, 2011, from EDGAROnline: http://sec.edgar-online.com/magna-international-inc/6-k-report-of-foreign-issuer/2003/06/23/section3.aspx.

37. Edgar Online. (June 30 2009). *Magna International Inc*. Retrieved May 7, 2011, from Edgaronline: http://sec.edgar-online.com/magna-international-inc/6-k-report-of-foreign-issuer/2009/06/30/section3.aspx.

38. EEOC. (2007). *EEOC and Walgreens resolve lawsuit*. Washington: U.S. equal employment opportunity commission.

39. Egelko, B. (June 1, 2011). "CVS to pay $55,000 to settle bias case." Retrieved June 29, 2001, from SFGate.com: http://www.sfgate.com/business/article/CVS-to-pay-55-000-to-settle-bias-case-2370006.php.

40. eHow. (2013). What Organizations Use ISO 9000. Retrieved on November 9, 2013 from eHow.com: http://www.ehow.com/info_8439852_organization-use-iso-9000__html.

41. Encarta. (2007). Thesaurus, Dictionary. *Microsoft Office 2007*. Encarta.

42. eNotes. (2011). *Leveraged Buyouts*. Retrieved November 12, 2011, from eNotes: http://www.enotes.com/leveraged-buyouts-reference/leveraged-buyouts-178583.

43. Filippelli, R. L. (1984). *Labor in the USA*. New York: Alfred A. Knopf.

44. Automotive Task Force. (2009). ISO/TS 16949:2009E. Quality Management Systems, Geneva, Switzerland.

45. Gaskin, Shelly, Robert Ferrett, Alicia Vargas, Carolyn McLellan. (2008). *GO! With Microsoft Office 2007 Introductory*. Upper Saddle River, New Jersey: Prentice Hall.

46. General Mills. (2008). *Corporate Social Responsibility 2008*. Retrieved September 28, 2009, from http://www.generalmills.com/corporate/commitment/newcsr2008.pdf.

47. General Mills. (2009). *Commitment-Values*. Retrieved September 28, 2009, from http://www.generalmills.com/corporate/commitment/values.aspx.

48. Glazer, Nathan. (2013). Wikipedia, Nathan Glazer biography. Retrieved September 6, 2013, from Wikipedia, the free encyclopedia: http://en.wikipedia.org/wiki/Nathan_Glazer.

49. Greenbaum, Joshua. (September 2010. Closing the Training Gap (Part 1). *Managing Automation*, p. 12.

50. Greenbaum, Joshua. (2013). EAConsult-Joshua Greenbaum biography. Retrieved September 12, 2013 from EAConsult: http://www.eaconsult.com/bio.html.

51. Guralnik, D. B. (1980). *Webster's New World Dictionary of American Language.* New York: Simon and Schuster.

52. Hachey, Sarah. (2008). Opening Quote – Lesson 2. Retrieved March 6, 2014, from http://www.in.gov/judiciary/citc/files/opening-quote.pdf.

53. Hamilton, C. (November 25, 2009). *Wal-Mart, family settle deadly prescription lawsuit*. Retrieved June 28, 2011, from Cecil Whig: http://www.cecilwhig.com/news/article/_8cde2775-50a2-5819-bb6e-991b358602bc.html.

54. Harshberger, Martin. (January 31, 2010). *Can Merger & Acquisitions Work?* Measurable Results, LLC. Retrieved November 4, 2011, from Website 101: http://website101.com/small-business/can-merger-acquisition-work.

55. HHS. (2009). U.S. Department of Health and Human Services. http://www.hhs.gov/ocr/civilrights/resources/laws/index.html. Accessed November 9, 2009.

56. Hines, A. (June 21, 2007). *Now Boarding: Southwest Airlines Goes International*. Retrieved August 8, 2010, from bnet: http://www.bnet.com/blog/intercom/now-boarding-southwest-airlines-goes-international/379.

57. Hoffman, A. (April 20, 1997). *Mend Affirmative Action: Attack the problem, Promote Diversity*. Retrieved June 15, 2011, from Summation: Auren Hoffman: http://www.summation.net/affirmative.html.

58. Hoover. (December 12, 2009). *Southwest Airlines*. Retrieved August 7, 2010, from Answers.com: http://www.answers.com/topic/southwest-airlines-co.

59. IMPO. (June 17, 2011). *GM To Invest $65 Million in N.Y., Tenn. Plants*. Retrieved June 17, 2011, from IMPO: http://www.impomag.com/news/2011/06/gm-invest-65-million-ny-tenn-plants.

60. US Legal, Inc. (2008). *Just Cause Law and Legal Definition*. http://definition.uslegal.com/j/just-cause/ Accessed November 9, 2009.

61. Investopedia. (2011). *Employee Buyout-EBO*. Retrieved November 4, 2011, from Investopedia: http://www.investopedia.com/terms/e/ebo.asp.

62. Jantsch, J. (June 24, 2010). *Small Business Marketing Blog from Duct Tape Marketing*. Retrieved August 7, 2010, from Duct Tape Marketing: http://www.ducttapemarketing.com/blog/2010/06/24/a-referral-ezxample-from-southwest-small-business-marketing.

63. Jantz, A., J. Baker, &M. Zabel (October 8, 2009). *General Mills: The Company of Champions*. Research Paper Cardinal Stritch University. Milwaukee, WI.

64. Jenifer S. Mueller University of Pennsylvania Wharton School of Management.

65. Jones, Gareth, Jennifer George. (2009). Contemporary Management. New York: McGraw-Hill Irwin.

66. Lemons, D., M. O'Kane, &A. Wurth (2005), *Next Generation Human Resources*: *Driving Organizational Excellence*. Houston, Texas: APQC.

67. King, D. R. (2004). Meta-analyses of Post-acquisition Performance: Indications of Unidentified Moderators. *Strategic Management Journal*, pp. 187–200.

68. King, D. R. (2008). Performance implications of firm resource interactions in the acquisition of R & D-intensive firms. *Organization Science*, pp. 327–340.

69. Kotler, Philip. (2009). *Marketing Management*. Upper Saddle River, New Jersey: Pearson Prentice Hall.

70. Krajewski, Lee, Larry P. Ritzman, Manoj K. Malhotra, (2010). *Operations Management*. Upper Saddle River, New Jersey: Prentice Hall.

71. Kreitner, R. (2010). *Organizational Behavior*. New York: McGraw-Hill.

72. Lamoreaux, N. R. (1985). *The great merger movement in American business*. Cambridge England: Cambridge University.

73. Peter, Laurence, Raymond Hull. (1987). *The Peter Principle*. New York: William Morrow and Company, Inc.

74. Leger, L. D. (June 11, 2013). Walgreens to pay $80 million for oxycodone violations. Retrieved March 8, 2014, from http://www.usatoday.com/story/news/nation/2013/06/11/walgreens-drug-oxycodone-license-80-million/2412451/.

75. Lombardi, Vince (1913–1970). Effort Quotation, Retrieved October 22, 2013, from Think Exist.com: http://thinkexist.com/quotes/vince_lombardi.

76. Lowe, Samantha. (2013). Types of Work Shift Schedules. Retrieved November 23, 2013, from eHow.com: http://www.ehow.com/list_5790170_types-work-shift-schedules.html.

77. Lundin, W., K. Lundin (1993). The Healing Manager. San Francisco: Berrett-Koehler.

78. Madland, David, Karla Walter (December 7, 2011). *Boeing-Machinist Deal Benefits Company, Workers, and NLRB Credibility*. Retrieved July 29, 2013 from Center for American Progress Action Fund:

http://www.americanprogressaction.org/issues/general/news/2011/12/07/10843/boeing-machinists-deal -benefits-company-workers-and-nlrb-credibility.

79. Magna International. (2011). *About Magna Powertrain-Powertrain Systems | Magna International Inc.* Retrieved April 22, 2011, from Magna: http://www.magna.com/xchg/powertrain_systems/XSL/standard.xsl/-/content/40_181.htm?rdeLocaleAttr=en.

80. Magna International. (2011). *Investors-Magna International Inc.* Retrieved April 22, 2011, from Magna International Investor: http://phx.corporate-ir.net/External.file?item=UGFyZW50SUQ9NDE5OTE zfENoaWxkSUQ9NDMzMjk5fFR5cGU9MQ==&t=1.

81. Magna International. (2011). *Our History*. Retrieved April 22, 2011, from Our History-Magna International Inc.: http://www.magna.com/magna/en/about/history/default.aspx.

82. Mathis, L. Robert, H. John Jackson (1991). *Personnel/Human Resource Management.*USA: West Publishing Corporation.

83. Mathis, L. Robert, H. John Jackson (1994). *Human Resource Management.*USA: West Publishing Corporation.

84. Mayne, E. M. (March 1, 2001). *Magna Stumbles Over Blackwood*. Retrieved July 3, 2011, from Ward's AutoWorld: http://waw.wardsauto.com/ar/auto_magna_stumbles_blackwood.

85. McDonald's. (2013). McDonalds, I'm Lovin' It. Retrieved December 14, 2013, from About McDonalds. com: http://www.aboutmcdonalds.com/mcd/newsroom/electronic_press_kits/mcdonalds_ usa_ commitments_to_offer_improved_nutrition_choices.html.

86. McLaughlin, David, Chris Dolmetsch (2012). NY Attorney General Says More Suits Will Follow JPMorgan. Retrieved December 12, 2013, from Bloomberg com: http://www.bloomberg.com/ news/2012-10-01/jpmorgan-sued-by-n-y-for-fraud-over-mortgage-securities.html.

87. Media, N. T. (August 15, 2007). *Senior Discounts Easy to Find at Southwest Airlines, Big Savings Online Now*. Retrieved August 8, 2010, from Senior Journal: http://www.senirjournal.com/news/discount/2007/7-08-15-sendiscountseasy.htm.

88. Mello, J. A. (2011). *Strategic Human Resource Management.* Mason, OH: South-Western Cengage Learning.

89. Monitor. (2008, 3 26). *CVS Caremark to pay $36.7M to settle fraud allegations*. Retrieved June 28, 2011, from HCPro: http://hcpro.com/CCP-208206-862/CVS=Caremark-to-pay-367M -to-settle-fruad-allegations.

90. Monitor. (June 11, 2008). *Walgreens to pay $35 million to settle fraud claims*. Retrieved 6 28, 2011, from HCPro: http://www.hcpor.com/CCP-213140-862/Walgreens-to-pay-35-million -to-settle-fraud-claims.

91. Monroe, W. Karmin. (1987). *Will the U.S. Stay Number One*. U.S. News and World Report, February issue.

92. Murrell, N. (April 11, 2011). *What Areas Do IQ Tests Assess?* Retrieved June 24, 2011, from eHow Family: http://www.ehow.com/info_8204470_areas-do-iq-tests-assess.html.

93. NCEO. (1993). *Employee Ownership Companies Pay Less for Workers' Compensation Costs.* Retrieved December 10, 2011, from NCEO: http://nceo.org/main/article.php/id/19.

94. NCEO. (2011). *Employee Stock Ownership Plans (ESOPs).* Retrieved November 12, 2011, from The National Center for Employee Ownership: http://www.nceo.org/main/articlelist.php.

95. Net Duty. (2013). Web Based Time Tracking. Retrieved November 23, 2013, from netDuty.com: http://www.dutycalendar.com/time-attendance.

96. netHelper. (2011). *Mergers and Acquisitions.* Retrieved December 2, 2011, from netHelper: http://www.nethelper.com/article/Mergers_and_Acquisitions.

97. Newswire. (May 23, 2011). *HDNet's Dan Rather Reports Explores the State of Public Education in the U.S.* Retrieved June 15, 2011, from PR Newswire: http://finance.yahoo.com/news/HDNets-Dan-Rather-Reports-prnews-1211761156.html?x=0&.v=1.

98. Newswire. (October 2, 2009). *CIGNA Corp.'s John M. Murabito Named 2009 HR Executive of the Year.* Retrieved June 28, 2011, from PR Newswire: http://www.prnewswire.com/news-release/cigna-corp-john-m-murabito-named-2009-HR-executive-of-the year. –

99. NIU Human Resource. (2004). AADR. Retrieved October 29, 2009, from http://www.hr.niu.edu/ServiceAreas/DiversityResources/Complaints.cfm.

100. OCAI. (2011). *Organizational Culture Types.* Retrieved June 14, 2011, from OCAI online: http://ocai-online.com/about-the-organizational-culture-Assessment-Instrument-OCAI/Organizational-Culture-Assessment-Instrument.

101. Olive Garden. (2013). About Us-Culinary Institute of Tuscany. Retrieved November 8, 2013, from Olive Garden.com: http://www.olivegarden.com/About-Us/Culinary-Institute-of-Tuscany.

102. Osteen, Joel. (2012). *I Declare.* New York, NY: FaithWords Hachette Book Group. p. 110.

103. Parr, W. (January 27, 2009). *Don't Punish Employees with Training.* Retrieved June 27, 2011, from Quality Magazine: http://www.qualitymag.com/Article/Article_Rotation?BNP_GUID_9-5-2006_A_1.

104. Pearce, I. A. (2011). *Strategic Management.* New York: McGraw-Hill.

105. Pletz, J. (December 1, 2009). *Bulldozing Pharmacy Benefit Manger, Caterpillar Engineers Drug Cost Savings.* Retrieved June 30, 2011, from Workforce Management: http://www.workforce.com/section/news/article/bulldozing-pharmacy-benefit-managers-caterpillar-engineers_printer.php.

106. Plunkert, Lois M. (1990). The 1980s: a decade of job growth and industry shifts. Retrieved October 3, 2013, from The Free Library: http://www.thefreelibrary.com/The+19801980's%a+a+decade+of+job+growth+and+industry+shift.

107. Quality. (2011). *Quality management: quality leadership 100*. Retrieved June 27, 2011, from Quality Magazine: http://www.qualitymag.com/Article/Department/BNP_Guid_9-5-2006_A1000(n.d.).

108. Rao, M. S. (January 23, 2009). *Where Knowledge is Wealth*. Retrieved June 24, 2011, from Profmsr. Blogspot: http://profmsr.blogspot.com/2009/01/motivation-vs-inspiration.html.

109. Reid, R. Dan. (2010). First Common Quality Standard. Retrieved December 15, 2013, from GM Heritage Center, Generation of GM History: http://history.gmheritagecenter.com/wiki/index.php/First_Common_Quality_Standard.

110. Marco, M. (June 21, 2007). *Jury Awards Walmart Pharmacist $2 Million In Sex-Discrimination Suit*. Retrieved September 19, 2016, from Consumerist: https://consumerist.com/2007/06/21/jury-awards-walmart-pharmacist-2-million-in-sex-discrimination-suit/

111. Shane, S. (April 28, 2008). *Startup Failure Rate-The REAL Number*. Retrieved December 10, 2011, from Small Biz Trends: http://smallbiztrends.com/2008/04/startup-failure-rate.html.

112. Solis, Hilda L. (2009). Office of Federal Contract Compliance Programs. Accessed November 9, 2009. http://www.dol.gov/ofccp/TAguides/SBguide.htm.

113. Song, K. (June 8, 2011). *Boeing's South Carolina move gets even more political*. Retrieved June 11, 2011, from The Seattle Times: http://seattletimes.nwsource.com/html/businesstechnology/2015269434_boeingnlrb09m.html.

114. Southwest. (2010). *What is a Ding?* Retrieved August 15, 2010, from http://www.southwest.com/ding/.

115. Southwest Airlines. (2008). *The Customer Zone*. Dallas: Southwest Airlines Co.

116. NCGE. (2011). *North Carolina in the Global Economy*. Retrieved June 19, 2011, from Center on Globalization, Governance & Competitiveness: http://www.soc.duke.edu/NC_GlobalEconomy/furniture/overview.shtml.

117. Staff, Business Management Systems. (2012). 2-2 3-2 2-3 Rotating Shift Schedule. Retrieved December 14, 2013, from Business Management System: http://community.bmscentral.com/learnss/ZC/c4tr12-4.

118. Staff, CSA. (2012). Wal-Mart centralizes compliance and legal issues. Retrieved March 8, 2014, from http://chainstoreage.com/article/wal-mart-centralizes-compliance-and-legal-issues.

119. Staff, Farlex (2014). Wagner Act. Retrieved March 8, 2014, from http://legal-dictionary.thefreedictionary.com/Wagner+Act.

120. Taylor, Fred, Jr. (2008). How Southwest's Culture Drives Cost Leadership. *OPG Business Leadership Program*. Hoenderloo, Netherlands: OPG. p. 21.

121. TC, V. M. (2011). *The Company Executive Summary*. Racine: XYZ.

122. Thomas. (April 27, 2011). *5 Top Trends in Venture Capital Today.* Retrieved December 10, 2011, from Growth Science: http://growthsci.com/blog/5_top_vc_trends.

123. Traub, James (2013). Wikipedia, James Traub biography. Retrieved September 6, 2013, from Wikipedia, the free encyclopedia: http://en.wikipedia.org/wiki/James_Traub.

124. Turek, Bob. (1994). Lean Manufacturing From The Performance Advantage: http://www.ehow.com/lean-manufacturing.

125. UPS History. (2013). UPS Corporate. Retrieved December 14, 2013, from UPS Corporate: http://www.ups.com/content/us/en/about/history/1990.html?WT.svl=SubNav.

126. Useem, J. (June 1, 2006). How to build a great team. Fortune Magazine http://money.cnn.com/2006/05/31/magazines/fortune/intro_greatteams_fortune_061206/index.htm.

127. US Legal, Inc. (2008). *Just Cause Law and Legal Definition.* http://definition.uslegal.com/j/just-cause/Accessed November 9, 2009.

128. US Office of Personnel Management. (2009). *Guidelines for Conducting Diversity Training.* Accessed November 9, 2009.http://www.opm.gov/hrd/lead/policy/diver97.asp.

129. Valentine, Debra, A. (June 25, 2007). The Evolution of U.S. Merger Law: Prepared Remarks of Debra A. Valentine. Retrieved October 17, 2013, from Federal Trade Commission: http://www.ftc.gov/speeches/other/dvperumerg.shtm.

130. Verschoor, C. C. (January 15, 2011). *How an embezzler stole millions from a small company.* Retrieved September 4, 2011, from The Free Library: http://www.thefreelibrary.com/How+an+employee+embezzler+stole+millions+from+a+small+company.a0246717491.

131. Waalace, J. (October 27, 2008). *Boeing and Aerospace News.* Retrieved June 11, 2011, from Seattle pi:http://blog.seattlepi.com/aerospace/2008/10/27/details-\now-boeing-strike-settlement-reached/.

132. WAHM. (2013). Work at Home Jobs. Retrieved November 13, 2013, from WAHM.com: http://www.wahm.com/jobs.html.

133. Wal-Mart. (January 15, 2011). *Leading with Integrity.* Retrieved June 28, 2011, from Wal-Mart Statement of Ethics: http://ethics.walmartstores.com/StatementOfEthics/RaiseAConcern.aspx.

134. Walgreens. (November 23, 2009). *Walgreens Names Kathleen Wilson-Thompson Senior Vice President and Chief Human Resources Officer.* Retrieved June 28, 2011, from Walgreens: http://news.walgreens.com/article_print.cfm?article_id=5237.

135. Warner, J. (October 1, 2001). *Inside Boeing's Big Move (Harvard Business Review).* Retrieved June 11, 2011, from M.R. Press Consulting: http://mrpressconsulting.com/articleboeing.php.

136. Wells, W. L. (September 2007). Transforming Worker Representation: The Magna Model in Canada and Mexico. Retrieved May 15, 2011, from Labour/Le Travail.

137. Wesley, Ken. (2013). LinkedIn, Vice-president-Workforce Planning & Strategy, Supreme Dream Photography. Retrieved September 8, 2013, from LinkedIn: http://www.linkedin.com/pub/ken-wesley/7/77/a0a.

138. Wiki Answer. (2013). Retrieved September 7, 2013, from Wikianswer.com: http://wikianswer.com/Q/What_does_the_phrase_the_best_laid_plans_Of_Mice_and_Men_often_go_awary_mean.

139. Wikipedia. (2013). Wikipedia, the free encyclopedia. Retrieved October 2, 2013, from Wikipedia.org: http://en.wikipedia.org/wiki/Peter_Drucker.

140. Wikipedia. (2014). Wikipedia, the free encyclopedia. Retrieved March 8, 2014, from http://en.wikipedia.org/wiki/Jack_Welch.

141. Williams, R. J. (2010). *Financial Accounting.* New York: McGraw-Hill Irwin.

142. Yu, Chung-Hsien. (November 29, 2006). *Internet Marketing Analysis of Southwest Airlines.* Retrieved August 7, 2010, from Boston IIt: http://yubadboston.blogspot.com/2006/11/internet-marketing-analysis-of.html.

143. Zimmerman, J. L. (2009). *Accounting For Decision Making And Control.* New York: McGraw-Hill Irwin.